FLORENCE

COMPREHENSIVE TRAVEL GUIDE 2025

A Journey Through Culture, History, Cuisine and Hidden Gems in the Northeast of Tuscany Region, Italy: With Practical Information and Interactive Maps

BY

CLIFFORD SANTOS

© 2025 Clifford Santos. All rights reserved.

No part of this publication may be reproduced, distributed, or transmitted in any form or by any means, including photocopying, recording, or other electronic or mechanical methods, without the prior written permission of the author, except in the case of brief quotations embodied in critical reviews and certain other noncommercial uses permitted by copyright law. For permission requests, write to the publisher via the Author's central page.

Disclaimer:

This book is a work of the author's expertise and travel experiences. The views and opinions expressed within these pages are those of the author and do not necessarily reflect the official policy or position of any other agency, organization, employer, or company. While the author has made every effort to ensure that the information in this book was correct at the time of publication, the author does not assume and hereby disclaims any liability to any party for any loss, damage, or disruption caused by errors or omissions, whether such errors or omissions result from negligence, accident, or any other cause.

TABLE OF CONTENTS

Copyright..1
My Adventure In Florence...5
Benefits Of This Guide..7

Chapter 1 Introduction To Florence...10
1.1 History And Culture..10
1.2 Geography, Climate And Best Time To Visit.................................12
1.3 Overview Of Florence Neighborhoods...14
1.4 Local Customs And Etiquette..16

Chapter 2 Accommodation Options...19
2.1 Luxury Hotels In Central Florence..20
2.2 Budget-Friendly Hostels And Guesthouses....................................22
2.3 Boutique Hotels And Luxury Resorts...24
2.4 Apartment Rentals And Vacation Homes.......................................27
2.5 Unique Accommodations: Villas And Castles...............................30

Chapter 3 Transportation In Florence..33
3.1 Getting To Florence...33
3.2 Public Transport: Bus And Train..35
3.3 Taxis And Ride-Sharing Services...37
3.4 Cycling In Florence...39
3.5 Car Rentals And Driving Tips..41
3.6 Parking And Traffic Information...44

Chapter 4 Top 10 Must-See Attractions...47
4.1 Cathedral Of Santa Maria Del Fiore (Duomo)................................48
4.2 Uffizi Gallery..50
4.3 Ponte Vecchio...52
4.4 Accademia Gallery...54

4.5 Palazzo Pitti And Boboli Gardens..56
4.6 San Lorenzo Market...58
4.7 Oltrarno Neighborhood..60
4.8 Piazzale Michelangelo...62
4.9 Santa Croce Basilica..65
4.10 Florence Baptistery..67

Chapter 5 Hidden Gems And Local Favorites..69
5.1 Off-The-Beaten-Path Neighborhoods..69
5.2 Local Markets And Shopping Streets..71
5.3 Authentic Trattorias And Restaurants..73
5.4 Wine Bars And Enoteche...75
5.5 Secret Gardens And Parks...77

Chapter 6 Day Trips And Excursions..79
6.1 Siena And San Gimignano...80
6.2 Pisa And Lucca..83
6.3 Chianti Wine Region..85
6.4 Cinque Terre...88

Chapter 7 Art, Architecture, And History...90
7.1 Renaissance Art And Architecture...90
7.2 Medici Family And Their Legacy..92
7.3 Historical Landmarks And Monuments..94
7.4 Museums And Galleries...96
7.5 Street Art And Contemporary Culture...97

Chapter 8 Food And Wine..100
8.1 Traditional Tuscan Cuisine..100
8.2 Wine Tasting And Vineyard Tours..102
8.3 Local Markets And Food Shopping..105
8.4 Cooking Classes And Workshops...108

8.5 Gelato And Coffee Culture..110

Chapter 9 Practical Information And Travel Resources......................113
9.1 Maps And Navigation..113
9.2 Five Days Itinerary..116
9.3 Essential Packing List...118
9.4 Visa Requirements And Entry Procedures.................................... 121
9.5 Safety Tips And Emergency Contacts...124
9.6 Currency Exchange And Banking Services................................... 126
9.7 Language, Communication And Useful Phrases..........................129
9.8 Shopping And Souvenirs..131
9.9 Health And Wellness Centers..133
9.10 Useful Websites, Mobile Apps And Online Resources.............135
9.11 Internet Access And Connectivity..137
9.12 Visitor Centers And Tourist Assistance.......................................140

Chapter 10 Events And Festivals... 143
10.1 Overview Of Florence's Events And Festivals...........................143
10.2 Must-Attend Events..146
10.3 Hidden Gems Of Events And Festivals.......................................148
10.4 Cultural Events And Exhibitions..151
10.5 Music And Dance Events..154
Conclusion And Recommendations... 157

MY ADVENTURE IN FLORENCE

Florence is not just a city; it is a living, breathing masterpiece. From the moment my feet touched its cobblestone streets, I felt as though I had stepped into a vibrant painting. Every corner of Florence seemed to whisper stories of art, history, and unparalleled beauty. As a seasoned traveler and author, I have visited countless places, but Florence possesses a magic that lingers in your soul long after you've left. The morning I arrived in Florence was one of those golden Italian mornings when the sun casts a warm glow over everything it touches. My first glimpse of the city came as I crossed the Ponte Vecchio, Florence's iconic medieval bridge. Its charming jumble of jewelry shops perched over the Arno River looked like a scene from a fairy tale. The air was filled with the faint clinking of artisan tools and the aroma of freshly brewed espresso wafting from nearby cafés. I wandered aimlessly through narrow streets, feeling the cool shade of stone walls that had stood for centuries. Each turn seemed to reveal another treasure – a quaint piazza, a hidden garden, or an intricately adorned church. Florence seemed to welcome me with open arms, its charm both humbling and intoxicating.

Standing in Piazza del Duomo was like being transported to another world. The grandeur of the Cathedral of Santa Maria del Fiore, with its massive red-tiled dome designed by Brunelleschi, took my breath away. I remember running my fingers along the intricate marble façade, feeling the craftsmanship and dedication that had gone into creating this wonder. Climbing to the top of the dome was a moment of pure awe. As I ascended the steep, narrow staircase, I marveled at the frescoes of The Last Judgment painted on the dome's interior. At the summit, Florence unfolded before me – a sea of terracotta roofs, rolling hills in the distance, and the Arno River snaking through the city. It was a view that brought tears to my eyes, not from sadness but from the sheer beauty of it all. Florence is synonymous with art, and no trip here is complete without a pilgrimage to the Uffizi Gallery. I spent hours wandering through its halls, utterly captivated by Botticelli's The Birth of Venus and Leonardo da Vinci's Annunciation. Each painting seemed alive, the stories they told timeless and poignant. But it wasn't just the galleries that impressed me; art spills out into the streets of Florence. I stumbled upon street performers sketching breathtaking portraits, musicians filling the air with classical melodies, and sculptures adorning almost every corner. The city itself is a canvas, and its artists continue to leave their mark on it.

As someone who believes in immersing myself fully in a culture, food plays an integral role in my travels. Florence did not disappoint. One of my most cherished memories was dining at a small, family-run trattoria tucked away in a quiet alley. The first bite of bistecca alla Fiorentina, a perfectly cooked T-bone steak, was nothing short of a revelation. Paired with a glass of Chianti wine, the flavors danced on my palate, rich and robust. I ended the meal with a serving of gelato, its creamy sweetness a perfect ending to an already magical evening. Every meal in Florence was an experience. From sipping espresso at a café in Piazza della Signoria to savoring fresh pasta at Mercato Centrale, I discovered that food here is not just sustenance; it is an art form that tells a story of tradition and passion. As night fell, Florence transformed. The crowds thinned, and the city took on a serene, almost mystical quality. I strolled along the Arno River, the reflections of the city lights dancing on the water. The Ponte Vecchio, illuminated against the dark sky, looked even more enchanting. One of my most unforgettable experiences was watching the sunset from Piazzale Michelangelo. As the sky blazed with hues of orange and pink, the city below seemed to glow. It was a moment of quiet reflection, a time to simply be present and marvel at the beauty of life.

What truly sets Florence apart, however, is its people. Warm, welcoming, and passionate, the Florentines are the heart and soul of their city. I met an elderly shop owner who shared stories of his family's history in Florence, a tour guide who spoke of art with tears in her eyes, and a young artist who dreamed of leaving her mark on the city's rich tapestry. Their love for their city was infectious, and their pride reminded me that Florence is not just a place to visit – it is a place to cherish. Leaving Florence was bittersweet. As I boarded the train, I couldn't help but glance back at the city that had given me so much in such a short time. Florence is a city that doesn't just show you its treasures – it invites you to become a part of them.

BENEFITS OF THIS GUIDE

This guide is designed to enhance your experience. From awe-inspiring museums and architectural marvels to delicious food and scenic strolls, Florence offers a perfect blend of historical depth and modern vibrancy. With this guide, you will be well-equipped to discover Florence's many layers and immerse yourself in its artistic and cultural brilliance.

Maps and Navigation: Florence's narrow, cobbled streets and piazzas can be a maze, but with the help of this guide, you'll navigate the city like a local. It includes detailed maps and information on digital navigation tools like Google Maps and Florence-specific apps, making it easier to plan your route, whether on foot or using public transport. You will find tips on pedestrian-friendly areas, key landmarks, and hidden gems, all accessible from Florence's city center, ensuring you never miss a beat while exploring this captivating city.

Accommodation Options: Florence offers a wide range of accommodation to suit all budgets. Luxury seekers can indulge in iconic hotels like the Hotel Savoy or the Four Seasons, while boutique inns in the Oltrarno district provide intimate, artistic settings. Budget travelers can find affordable hostels and guesthouses near the historic center, and vacation rentals offer a chance to live like a local. With recommendations across price points and neighborhoods, you'll find the perfect place to stay, whether you're seeking luxury, simplicity, or a home away from home.

Transportation: Florence's compact size makes walking the most enjoyable and convenient way to explore the city, but the guide also covers public transportation options. The city's ATAF buses can take you to less central areas, and taxis are available for quicker trips or when you need to rest your feet. The central train station, Santa Maria Novella, is a hub for day trips to other Tuscan cities and beyond. Cycling is another popular choice, with bike rental shops throughout the city, allowing you to explore Florence from a different perspective.

Top Attractions: Florence is home to some of the world's most celebrated art and architecture, and this guide ensures you don't miss a single highlight. The Duomo, with its iconic dome by Brunelleschi, is a must-see, along with the Uffizi Gallery, housing masterpieces by Botticelli and Michelangelo. The Ponte Vecchio offers scenic views of the Arno River, while the Pitti Palace and Boboli

Gardens offer a glimpse into Florence's royal past. For a truly unique experience, the guide also takes you off the beaten path to lesser-known gems, ensuring a well-rounded visit.

Culinary Delights: Florence's culinary scene is a feast for the senses, and this guide provides recommendations that take you from traditional trattorias to bustling markets. Indulge in local dishes like the famous Bistecca alla Fiorentina or Ribollita, or discover street food like lampredotto at Mercato Centrale. Florence is also renowned for its wine, particularly Chianti, and the guide includes information on where to enjoy tastings and wine pairings. Whether you're seeking a fine dining experience or a quick bite, this guide will help you savor the essence of Florence through its food.

Culture and Heritage: Florence's cultural heritage is a cornerstone of its identity, and this guide takes you deep into the heart of the city's Renaissance legacy. With its world-class museums, including the Uffizi and Accademia Gallery, Florence offers an unparalleled opportunity to view the works of masters like Leonardo da Vinci, Michelangelo, and Raphael. The city's architecture, from the Florence Cathedral to the Palazzo Vecchio, tells the story of Florence's evolution as a center of art and power. This guide provides insights into Florence's rich history and offers suggestions for exploring its cultural landmarks and hidden treasures.

Outdoor Activities and Adventures: While Florence is known for its art and history, it also offers a variety of outdoor activities for nature lovers and adventure seekers. The Boboli Gardens provide a peaceful retreat, offering beautiful landscapes and stunning views of the city. For those looking for more active pursuits, hiking trails around Fiesole or a bike ride along the Arno River present opportunities to experience the natural beauty of Tuscany. The guide also suggests day trips to nearby Tuscan towns for those seeking to further immerse themselves in the region's scenic charm.

Shopping: Florence is a shopper's paradise, whether you're hunting for high-end designer goods or one-of-a-kind artisan pieces. The guide provides a thorough overview of Florence's shopping districts, from the luxury boutiques along Via de' Tornabuoni to the artisanal shops of the Oltrarno district. Discover handcrafted leather goods, handmade jewelry, and intricate Florentine paper at local markets. Whether you're looking for a chic souvenir or a designer fashion statement, this guide will help you find the perfect items to take home.

Day Trips and Excursions: Florence's central location makes it an ideal base for exploring the rest of Tuscany and beyond, and this guide offers suggestions for unforgettable day trips. Visit the medieval city of Siena, the iconic Leaning Tower of Pisa, or the charming hilltop town of San Gimignano. For wine lovers, the Chianti region offers scenic vineyards and exquisite tastings. Whether you're traveling by train, bus, or car, this guide ensures that you can explore Tuscany's surrounding areas with ease, offering the perfect mix of adventure and relaxation.

Entertainment and Nightlife: Florence may be known for its historical significance, but its nightlife scene is vibrant and varied. The guide highlights the best wine bars, cocktail lounges, and nightclubs in the city, from the cozy Enoteca Pinchiorri to the lively spaces of the Oltrarno district. For live music lovers, Florence offers intimate jazz clubs and classical performances at venues like the Teatro Verdi. Whether you're seeking a quiet evening sipping wine or a night of dancing, Florence's nightlife offers something for everyone.

Practical Information and Travel Resources: This guide also provides essential practical information to ensure a smooth and stress-free visit. You'll find tips on local customs and etiquette, emergency contact numbers, and advice on currency exchange and tipping practices. With useful travel resources like ticketing information for popular attractions and advice on how to avoid crowds, this guide ensures that you can make the most of your time in Florence. It also includes packing recommendations tailored to Florence's seasons, helping you prepare for your trip with ease.

CHAPTER 1
INTRODUCTION TO FLORENCE

1.1 History and Culture

Florence, a city where the past lingers in every stone and the spirit of its history can still be felt in the air, holds an extraordinary legacy that has shaped not only Italy but the entire world. The origin of Florence dates back to Roman times, but its story truly begins to unfold in the Middle Ages, around the 12th century, when it started to emerge as a powerful and influential city-state. As you walk through its streets, you will discover that Florence is much more than a place; it is a living testament to a civilization that laid the foundations for art, culture, and human achievement. The city's rise began during the early Middle Ages, when it was a small Roman settlement known as Florentia. It was initially a military and trading outpost, but over time, it grew into a flourishing center of commerce and craftsmanship. Florence's location along the Arno River made it an ideal hub for trade, attracting merchants and craftsmen from across Europe. By the 11th century, its role as a center of banking and finance had been solidified, with its growing wealth fueling the city's cultural and architectural transformation. It was during this period that Florence began to blossom as a beacon of innovation and creativity.

Florence's cultural evolution reached its zenith during the Renaissance, a period that not only changed the city but also the course of human history. The 14th and 15th centuries were a time when art, science, philosophy, and politics flourished in an unprecedented way. The Medici family, who rose to power in the early 15th century, played a pivotal role in shaping Florence's cultural landscape. As patrons of the arts, the Medici family fostered an environment where artists like Leonardo da Vinci, Michelangelo, and Botticelli could develop their craft. It was here, in the heart of Florence, that the world witnessed the creation of masterpieces that would define Western art for centuries to come. The cultural legacy of Florence is not just found in its paintings and sculptures but in the very fabric of the city itself. Landmarks like the Florence Cathedral, with its stunning dome designed by Filippo Brunelleschi, stand as symbols of the ingenuity and ambition that characterized the Renaissance. The city's museums, including the Uffizi Gallery and the Accademia, house some of the most iconic works of art, drawing visitors from across the globe who come to experience the genius of the past. But Florence's heritage isn't limited to art alone. Its influence on literature, philosophy, and political thought is also profound. Dante Alighieri, one of Italy's greatest poets and the author of The Divine Comedy, was born here, and his work continues to shape the cultural discourse of the city.

As you explore the streets of Florence, you can't help but feel the weight of its history. Walking through the Piazza del Duomo, where the majestic cathedral stands, it's impossible not to imagine the centuries of devotion and artistry that went into its construction. The piazza, located in the city's historic center, has been a hub of religious and civic life for over 700 years. Not far from here, in the Piazza della Signoria, you can stand before the imposing Palazzo Vecchio, which has served as the political heart of Florence since the Middle Ages. The city's rich history can also be seen in the many churches and palaces that line its streets, each one a testament to Florence's devotion to beauty, craftsmanship, and the pursuit of knowledge. Florence's cultural heritage continues to shape the lives of its residents today. The city is not just a living museum; it is a vibrant cultural center that hosts world-class events, festivals, and performances throughout the year. The Florence Opera House is home to some of Italy's most talented musicians and performers, while the annual Maggio Musicale Fiorentino festival celebrates the city's long-standing connection to the arts. Even the food in Florence carries a sense of history, with traditional dishes like ribollita (a hearty vegetable soup) and bistecca alla Fiorentina (Florentine-style steak) offering a taste of the past that has been passed down through generations.

While Florence has undeniably transformed over the centuries, its identity has remained rooted in the values that have always defined it: a love for art, a passion for intellectual pursuit, and an enduring commitment to beauty. Every visit to the city is an invitation to experience that history firsthand, to walk through its ancient streets, and to appreciate the timeless culture that continues to thrive in its museums, churches, and plazas. Florence is a city where the past is not just preserved but is a living, breathing part of everyday life, inviting visitors to connect with its rich heritage in a way that is both profound and personal. As I walked through Florence's streets, I was reminded of the city's ability to inspire. It is a place that encourages creativity, reflection, and admiration for the achievements of those who came before us. It is a city that reminds us of the importance of preserving culture, of honoring our history, and of continuously seeking to push the boundaries of human potential. For anyone seeking to experience the heart of Italy, to immerse themselves in a city where history and culture intertwine in the most captivating way, Florence is a destination like no other.

1.2 Geography, Climate and Best Time to Visit

Florence is surrounded by a landscape that has shaped its history, culture, and charm. The city lies on the banks of the Arno River, which flows east to west across the region. The Arno is not just a geographical feature but a lifeline that has witnessed centuries of Florentine history and played a vital role in the city's development as a cultural and economic powerhouse. To the north of Florence, the Apennine Mountains rise majestically, their presence offering a natural barrier that creates the city's unique climate. This geographical positioning gives Florence an enchanting balance of urban beauty, historical significance, and natural splendor. The surrounding Tuscan hills are dotted with vineyards, olive groves, and small, picturesque villages that offer visitors a glimpse of rural life. These hills are also a key element of the city's geography, providing a backdrop to Florence's skyline and contributing to its idyllic atmosphere. The city's urban layout is defined by its historic center, a UNESCO World Heritage site, where narrow streets, Renaissance palaces, and ancient churches create an enchanting blend of architectural and geographical beauty. Navigating Florence is a journey through time, and every corner of the city offers something for both the history lover and the nature enthusiast.

Climate of Florence: Florence experiences a Mediterranean climate, characterized by hot summers and mild, wet winters. The proximity to the Apennine Mountains and the surrounding hills helps temper the extremes of temperature, but the city can still experience notable seasonal shifts. Understanding Florence's climate is crucial for visitors looking to make the most of their time in the city, as the weather can significantly influence your travel experience.

Summer: Summer in Florence is long and hot, with temperatures often soaring above 30°C (86°F) in July and August. The city can become quite crowded during this peak tourist season, as travelers flock to experience its art, history, and culture under the summer sun. The heat can be intense, particularly in the city center, where the stone buildings and narrow streets retain heat. While summer evenings bring some relief, with temperatures dropping to more comfortable levels, the daytime heat can make outdoor activities like walking through the city or visiting gardens less enjoyable. Visitors during this season should be prepared for the heat and consider early morning or late afternoon outings to avoid the midday sun.

Autumn: Autumn, from September to November, is a wonderful time to visit Florence. The weather begins to cool down after the summer heat, and the city becomes less crowded as the peak tourist season wanes. September and October are particularly pleasant, with daytime temperatures ranging from 18°C to 25°C (64°F to 77°F), making it ideal for sightseeing and outdoor activities. The autumn foliage in the surrounding Tuscan hills also adds a beautiful touch to the cityscape, as the leaves turn shades of orange, red, and gold. Rain becomes more frequent in November, but the temperatures remain mild, allowing visitors to enjoy Florence's cultural offerings without the summer crowds. This season offers a perfect balance of pleasant weather and fewer tourists, making it a favorite among those who want to experience the city in a more relaxed atmosphere.

Winter: Winter in Florence, from December to February, is the quietest season for tourism. The city is cooler, with temperatures typically ranging from 3°C to 10°C (37°F to 50°F), but it rarely experiences freezing temperatures. Snow is a rare occurrence, though the mountains surrounding the city may be dusted with snow, creating a magical backdrop. The low temperatures make it less ideal for extensive outdoor exploration, but this is also when Florence's indoor attractions—such as museums, galleries, and historic churches—shine. Fewer tourists mean shorter lines and less crowded experiences, making winter a good time for art lovers and those who want to immerse themselves in the city's history without the distractions of large crowds. The Christmas season, especially in December, brings festive lights and events, creating a warm, cozy atmosphere in the city, despite the chill in the air.

Spring: Spring in Florence, from March to May, is one of the most enchanting times to visit. The weather begins to warm up, with daytime temperatures ranging from 10°C to 20°C (50°F to 68°F), and the city is bathed in the gentle warmth of the sun. The gardens of Florence, such as the Boboli Gardens and the rose garden in Piazzale Michelangelo, come alive with color as flowers bloom, filling the air with fragrance. Spring is also the season when many outdoor events and festivals take place, making it an exciting time to explore the city. The crowds are still manageable in the early spring, but by May, the city starts to see an increase in visitors, particularly towards the end of the month. However, the pleasant weather and vibrant atmosphere make this an ideal time to experience Florence's blend of history, culture, and nature.

Best Times to Visit Florence: The best time to visit Florence largely depends on what kind of experience you're seeking. For those who prefer warm weather, fewer crowds, and an abundance of outdoor activities, spring and autumn are the perfect seasons. These seasons offer comfortable temperatures, ideal for leisurely strolls through the city's historic center, visiting the Florence Cathedral, or enjoying a glass of wine in a café along the Arno River. The weather is also ideal for exploring the nearby Tuscan countryside, with its vineyards and olive groves that are particularly stunning in autumn. Summer, while lively and bustling, is best for visitors who thrive in a busy atmosphere and don't mind the heat. However, if you choose to visit Florence during the summer, it's important to plan your activities wisely—early morning or late afternoon are the best times to explore the city to avoid the peak heat and crowds. Winter, on the other hand, offers a quieter and more intimate experience. While some outdoor activities may be less pleasant, it is the ideal time for museum lovers and those seeking a slower-paced visit. The city's festive spirit during Christmas adds a special charm to the winter months, making it a magical time to visit for those who enjoy the holiday atmosphere.

1.3 Overview of Florence Neighborhoods
Each of Florence's neighborhoods offers a distinct experience, one that will leave you with a deeper understanding of the city's past and its ever-evolving present. Whether you're soaking in the history of the city center, experiencing the artisan traditions of the Oltrarno, or discovering the youthful energy of Santa Croce, Florence invites you to explore its many faces. Each corner of this

remarkable city holds a story waiting to be uncovered, and the neighborhoods are the perfect starting point for that journey.

The Historic Center: The historic center of Florence is where most travelers begin their journey, and it is impossible to miss its allure. This area is home to iconic landmarks such as the Duomo, the Uffizi Gallery, and the Ponte Vecchio. Yet, beyond the major attractions, the heart of the city pulses with life. As you wander through its narrow streets, you'll find charming cafes tucked in quiet squares, small shops selling artisanal goods, and a steady flow of Florentines going about their daily lives. The historic center feels alive with history, yet is dynamic, offering a perfect balance of culture, commerce, and art. It's here that you can walk in the footsteps of the great Renaissance masters, like Michelangelo and Leonardo da Vinci, as their works still adorn museums and buildings, creating a living legacy that's impossible to ignore.

Oltrarno: If you're seeking a neighborhood that offers a bit of peace while still being close to all the action, the Oltrarno district is the place to be. Located just across the Arno River from the historic center, the Oltrarno is often considered the more authentic side of Florence. Here, the pace of life slows down, and the essence of Florence's artisanal tradition comes to the forefront. As you stroll through its winding streets, you'll pass workshops where local craftsmen create everything from hand-carved leather goods to intricate metalwork. The area also boasts some of the most beautiful gardens and villas, such as the Boboli Gardens behind the Pitti Palace, which offers an escape from the hustle and bustle of the city. While the Oltrarno maintains its connection to Florence's past, it also has a creative and modern flair, with hip cafes, trendy galleries, and lively bars that make it a favorite spot for locals and savvy visitors alike.

San Frediano: For those who want to experience Florence from a more intimate and residential perspective, the San Frediano neighborhood is a must-visit. Located on the south side of the Arno River, it exudes a warmth and authenticity that many other areas of the city have lost to tourism. This residential area is dotted with small restaurants, family-owned trattorias, and charming piazzas. It's a wonderful place to discover Florentine life as it's lived away from the major tourist attractions. San Frediano is also known for its street art, with colorful murals adorning many of its buildings, adding a contemporary twist to the traditional architecture. Here, you can enjoy a coffee in one of the local cafes and watch the world go by, soaking in the true essence of Florence without the crowds. The neighborhood's charm lies in its simplicity and its ability to make you feel like you are part of the city's heartbeat.

Santa Croce: Just to the north of the city center, you'll find the lively and youthful Santa Croce district. Known for the iconic Basilica di Santa Croce, this neighborhood is alive with energy, thanks to the many students and young professionals who live and work here. The square in front of the basilica is a hub for cultural and social activities, with performances, outdoor markets, and festivals throughout the year. The area is also home to some of Florence's most interesting shops, from vintage stores to independent boutiques, where you can find one-of-a-kind fashion pieces and unique gifts. Santa Croce has an undeniably bohemian atmosphere, attracting a crowd that loves art, music, and the city's modern-day creativity. The vibrant nightlife, with its many pubs and music venues, makes it a great place to explore after dark, offering something for everyone from casual hangouts to late-night dancing.

San Giovanni: Finally, the San Giovanni district, where the Florence Cathedral is located, is often referred to as the spiritual heart of the city. The area is filled with a mix of religious sites, elegant piazzas, and Renaissance architecture, making it a must-see for history and culture enthusiasts. The famous Duomo, with its stunning dome by Brunelleschi, dominates the skyline and is a central point around which the rest of the neighborhood unfolds. This district is also home to some of Florence's finest shopping streets, with high-end boutiques and luxury stores lining Via de' Tornabuoni. Despite its fame and grandeur, the San Giovanni district also has quiet, charming corners, where you can step into cafes and enjoy a peaceful moment. The blend of historic grandeur and modern luxury here makes the district a fascinating place to visit, where you can find both timeless beauty and contemporary allure.

1.4 Local Customs and Etiquette

These local customs and etiquettes are not just formalities but represent the heart of what makes Florence so extraordinary. They offer visitors a way to connect with the city on a deeper level, to understand the values that have shaped its past, and to experience the daily life of its people. In Florence, you're not merely a traveler; you're invited to be part of a living tradition that continues to thrive and evolve, creating a space where art, culture, and human connection are always at the forefront.

Dining Etiquette: In Florence, dining is more than just a meal—it's a celebration of life, culture, and tradition. Food plays a central role in the lives of the Florentines, and the rituals surrounding it are deeply ingrained in the city's social fabric. When you sit down at a restaurant, it's customary to greet the waiter with a polite "buonasera" or "buongiorno," showing respect for the staff and the experience that awaits. Florentines take their time when eating, savoring every bite while engaging in conversation. It's important to wait until everyone at the table is served before you begin your meal. Furthermore, altering dishes or requesting modifications is often seen as disrespectful to the chef's craft. Florentines believe in the artistry of food, and their approach to dining reflects a commitment to quality and tradition.

Greetings and Social Interactions: One of the most striking customs in Florence is the warmth with which locals greet one another. Whether you're strolling through the vibrant Piazza della Signoria or wandering the quieter streets near the Arno River, it's common to exchange a friendly "ciao" or "salve" with even strangers. This culture of openness is not just a formality but a reflection of Florence's deep sense of community. When you ask for directions or recommendations, Florentines are eager to share their knowledge, often offering insider tips on lesser-known spots like artisan workshops in the Oltrarno district. Handshakes are common when meeting new people, accompanied by eye contact and a genuine smile, reinforcing the importance of personal connections in Florentine society.

Fashion and Appearance: Florence is renowned as one of Italy's fashion capitals, and its residents take great pride in their appearance. Walking through the elegant streets near Piazza della Repubblica or Via de' Tornabuoni, you'll notice that locals are always impeccably dressed, with an emphasis on refinement and style. For visitors, dressing well is not only appreciated but expected, especially when entering fine dining establishments or cultural landmarks like the Uffizi Gallery. While casual wear is perfectly acceptable for sightseeing, showing respect for the city's aesthetic values by dressing neatly is seen as a sign of respect. Florentines' attention to personal style reflects a broader cultural reverence for beauty, from the art and architecture to the way people carry themselves in daily life.

Religious Reverence: Florence's religious traditions are integral to its cultural identity, and visitors are expected to show reverence when visiting its sacred spaces. Churches like the Duomo or the Basilica di Santa Croce are not just places of worship but are steeped in centuries of history. When entering these religious sites, it is customary to dress modestly, covering shoulders and knees, in accordance with the city's long-standing respect for faith. During significant religious events, such as Easter or Christmas, the streets of Florence come alive with processions and celebrations that honor the city's Christian heritage. This deep connection to faith permeates the city's daily life, creating an atmosphere of reverence and spiritual continuity that visitors are encouraged to acknowledge and respect.

Calcio Storico: One of the most unique and exciting customs in Florence is the Calcio Storico, a centuries-old game that is still played today. Held annually in June in the Piazza Santa Croce, this medieval football match blends elements of rugby, soccer, and wrestling, and is an unforgettable spectacle of strength, strategy, and Florentine pride.

CHAPTER 2
ACCOMMODATION OPTIONS

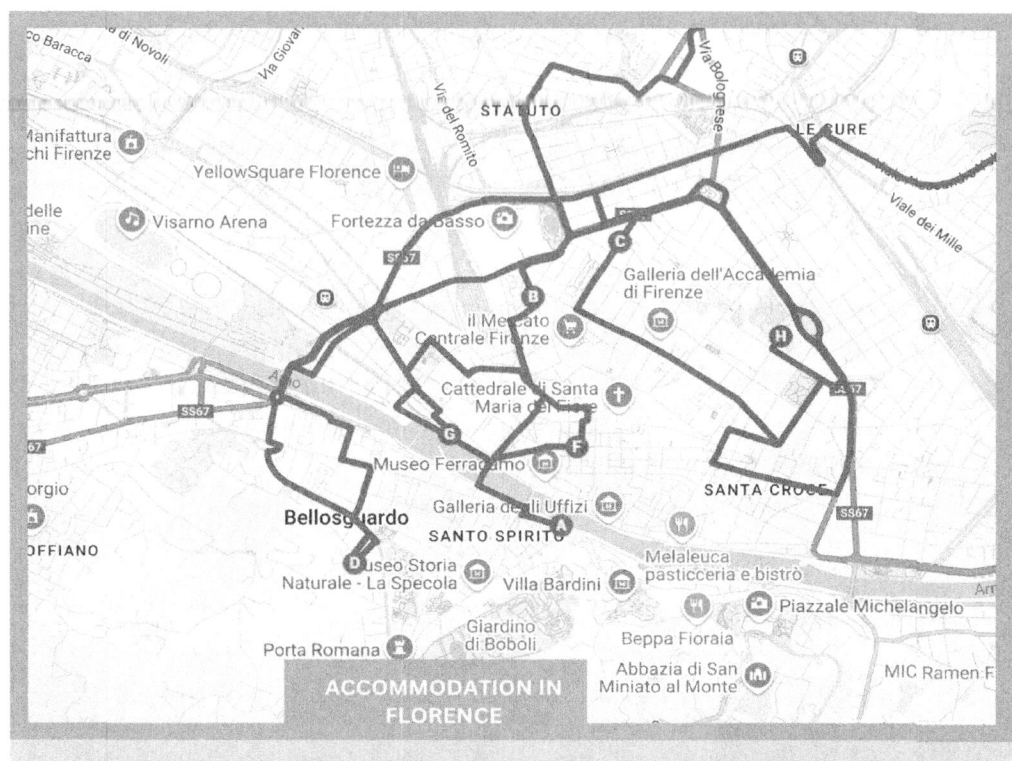

ACCOMMODATION IN FLORENCE

Directions from Florence, Italy to Hotel Savoy, Piazza della Repubblica, Florence, Metropolitan City of Florence, Italy

A
Florence, Italy

B
My Friends, Via Faenza, Florence, Metropolitan City of Florence, Italy

C
PLUS Florence, Via Santa Caterina D'Alessandria, Florence, Metropolitan City of Florence, Italy

D
Tasso Hostel, Via Villani, Florence, Metropolitan City of Florence, Italy

E
Belmond Villa San Michele, Via Doccia, Fiesole, Metropolitan City of Florence, Italy

F
Palazzo Vecchietti, Via degli Strozzi, Florence, Metropolitan City of Florence, Italy

G
The St. Regis Florence, Piazza Ognissanti, Florence, Metropolitan City of Florence, Italy

H
Four Seasons Hotel Firenze, Borgo Pinti, Florence, Metropolitan City of Florence, Italy

I
Hotel Savoy, Piazza della Repubblica, Florence, Metropolitan City of Florence, Italy

19

2.1 Luxury Hotels in Central Florence

These hotels are not just places to rest; they are experiences that blend opulence with history, sophistication with service, and Italian charm with international standards. In this essay, we explore five distinguished luxury hotels that define the hospitality scene in Florence, offering an array of unique features, unparalleled amenities, and exceptional services to enhance any visit.

Hotel Savoy: Situated at the very heart of Florence, the Hotel Savoy offers a refined blend of tradition and contemporary luxury. Located just steps from the iconic Duomo and the Uffizi Gallery, this hotel provides an unparalleled view of the city's artistic heritage. Its design effortlessly combines modern comfort with elegant Florentine decor, creating a serene atmosphere that is both stylish and inviting. Prices for rooms at Hotel Savoy typically start around €500 per night, with luxury suites reaching upwards of €1,200. Each room is equipped with high-end amenities such as plush bedding, state-of-the-art entertainment systems, and marble bathrooms. Guests can enjoy exquisite dining at the hotel's restaurant, Irene, which offers a modern take on traditional Tuscan cuisine, with meals averaging around €60-€100 per person. The hotel also provides personalized services, including private guided tours of Florence's most famous landmarks, a luxury shopping experience, and a wellness center with a fully equipped gym and a dedicated spa treatment area. For reservations, more details, and booking, guests can visit the hotel's official website at www.roccofortehotels.com.

Four Seasons Hotel Firenze: For those seeking an extraordinary experience steeped in history, the Four Seasons Hotel Firenze is an unrivaled choice. Housed in a former convent dating back to the 15th century, this hotel boasts a stunning location just outside the city's historic center, surrounded by lush gardens and close to Florence's main attractions. The Four Seasons offers a serene sanctuary amidst the hustle and bustle of the city. Room prices at the Four Seasons start from €800 per night, with suites reaching over €2,000. Each of the hotel's 116 rooms and suites reflects Renaissance-inspired design with modern luxury touches, featuring spacious layouts, antique furniture, and opulent marble bathrooms. The hotel's Michelin-starred restaurant, Il Palagio, serves some of the finest Tuscan cuisine, with meals averaging €120-€200 per person. Guests can also indulge in the spa and wellness services, including a tranquil outdoor pool, personalized massages, and beauty treatments. Additional services such as private art tours, personal shopping experiences, and exclusive cooking classes are available, ensuring that every guest receives a truly bespoke experience. For more information or to make a reservation, visitors can visit www.fourseasons.com.

The St. Regis Florence: The St. Regis Florence is a luxurious hotel set along the Arno River, offering guests an authentic Florentine experience in a palatial setting. Known for its refined elegance and exceptional service, the St. Regis is located just minutes from the famous Ponte Vecchio and the Florence Cathedral, making it an ideal base for exploring the city's treasures. With room rates starting at €600 per night, the St. Regis Florence caters to high-end clientele, offering suites that can exceed €2,500 per night. The rooms are furnished with luxurious fabrics, antique furniture, and modern amenities, ensuring comfort and style in every corner. Guests can dine at the hotel's celebrated restaurant, Winter Garden by Caino, where the price for meals averages between €80-€150 per person. The hotel's signature butler service is available to meet any request, whether it's securing a private tour of the Uffizi or arranging an exclusive fashion experience. Additionally, the St. Regis features a fully equipped fitness center and an indulgent spa, ensuring relaxation after a day of sightseeing. For more details and booking, guests can visit www.stregisflorence.com.

Palazzo Vecchietti: Palazzo Vecchietti offers an exclusive boutique hotel experience with the elegance and charm of a historic Florentine palazzo. Nestled in the heart of Florence, this luxurious hotel is just a short walk from the Duomo and the city's most prestigious museums. Palazzo Vecchietti is a unique fusion of contemporary luxury and classical Florentine design, providing an intimate atmosphere that makes each guest feel like a part of history. With room prices starting from €450 per night, Palazzo Vecchietti caters to those seeking understated elegance. The rooms are designed with a blend of classic and modern elements, offering spacious layouts, rich fabrics, and carefully curated artwork. The hotel's private butler service ensures a highly personalized experience, while the in-house restaurant serves delectable Tuscan dishes, with meals costing around €70-€120 per person. Guests can also enjoy the hotel's exclusive wellness services, including yoga and massage treatments in the privacy of their rooms. To reserve a room or learn more about the hotel, visit www.palazzovecchietti.com.

Belmond Villa San Michele: Set amidst the rolling hills of Fiesole, just a short drive from central Florence, Belmond Villa San Michele offers an idyllic escape with stunning views of the city and the Tuscan countryside. Housed in a former monastery, this luxurious hotel is a tranquil retreat that combines the charm of a historic building with modern comforts. Prices at Belmond Villa San Michele start at approximately €700 per night, with suites and villas available for upwards of €2,500. The rooms feature antique furniture, luxurious linens, and magnificent views of Florence and the surrounding hills. Guests can dine at the hotel's renowned restaurant, La Loggia, where traditional Tuscan cuisine is served in an elegant setting. Meals here typically range from €80 to €150 per person. Additionally, the hotel offers a wide array of services, such as cooking classes, wine tastings, and personalized tours of Florence and the Tuscan countryside. The spa offers a selection of treatments designed to pamper and rejuvenate guests after a day of exploration. For booking and more information, visitors can visit www.belmond.com.

2.2 Budget-Friendly Hostels and Guesthouses

Finding budget-friendly accommodation is key to enjoying all that Florence has to offer without breaking the bank. Luckily, the city boasts a wide range of hostels and guesthouses that cater to travelers looking for affordable, comfortable, and welcoming stays. In this essay, we will explore budget-friendly hostels and guesthouses in Florence, offering a glimpse into their location, amenities, prices, and unique features to help you choose the perfect place to stay on your trip to this vibrant city.

Ostello Tasso: Located in the San Frediano district, one of Florence's most authentic and artistic neighborhoods, Ostello Tasso offers a welcoming and lively environment for travelers on a budget. Known for its friendly atmosphere, this hostel is popular among backpackers and young travelers. The dormitory-style rooms are clean, spacious, and come with either shared or private bathrooms. Prices for a bed in a shared dorm start around €20-€25 per night, while private rooms begin at approximately €60 per night. The hostel offers free Wi-Fi, a communal kitchen, and a cozy common area where guests can relax, socialize, or enjoy a game of billiards. One of the standout features of Ostello Tasso is its proximity to the Arno River and the historic center, just a short walk away, allowing guests to easily explore Florence's main attractions such as the Ponte Vecchio and the Uffizi Gallery. Breakfast is available for an additional cost, and the friendly staff are always happy to provide local tips and recommendations. For reservations and more details, visit their official website at ostellotasso.com.

Hostel Gallo d'Oro: Just a few minutes from the Santa Maria Novella train station, Hostel Gallo d'Oro is an excellent option for budget-conscious travelers who want to be in the heart of Florence. With prices starting at €18 per night for a bed in a mixed dormitory and private rooms available from €45, Hostel Gallo d'Oro is known for its clean and functional rooms. It's a popular choice for travelers who appreciate a calm, no-frills atmosphere. The hostel offers free Wi-Fi, a large kitchen for guests to prepare their meals, and a lounge area with TV and board games. The warm, welcoming staff also organize free walking tours to help visitors explore the city, and the hostel has partnerships with local businesses, providing discounts for restaurants and attractions. A continental breakfast is available for an additional charge. With its central location, Hostel Gallo d'Oro allows guests to easily walk to Florence's major attractions such as the Duomo, Piazza della Signoria, and the Accademia Gallery. More information and bookings can be made at gallodoro.com.

Plus Florence: For those seeking a slightly more upscale but still affordable option, Plus Florence provides modern amenities and great value. Located in the Santa Maria Novella area, this hostel offers a range of room types, from dormitories to private rooms, with prices starting at €25 per night for a bed in a dorm. Private rooms can be booked starting at €70 per night. The property features an outdoor pool, a rooftop terrace, and a fitness center, making it an ideal place for travelers who want to enjoy a little extra comfort. The hostel also has a restaurant serving Italian and international cuisine, with meals priced around €8-€15. Plus Florence stands out for its clean, modern interiors and the large common areas, which include a bar and a social lounge where travelers can meet and relax. Additionally, the hostel offers laundry services, free Wi-Fi, and daily events to keep guests entertained. Whether you're exploring Florence's rich history or simply relaxing by the pool, Plus Florence is an excellent choice for those seeking a balance of affordability and comfort. For bookings and more details, visit their website at plusflorence.com.

My Friends Hostel: Located near the historic center of Florence, My Friends Hostel is a charming and budget-friendly option that caters to travelers seeking a more intimate, homely environment. The hostel offers both dormitory-style rooms and private rooms, with rates starting at €20 for a bed in a dorm and €50 for a private room. Guests can enjoy a range of amenities, including a fully equipped kitchen, free Wi-Fi, and a cozy common area perfect for socializing. The hostel has a reputation for its helpful and friendly staff, who are eager to assist with local recommendations and directions. My Friends Hostel is within walking distance of many of Florence's key attractions, including the famous Florence Cathedral and the lively San Lorenzo Market. A continental breakfast is included in the room price, and guests can enjoy a complimentary coffee or tea throughout the day. This hostel's intimate atmosphere and central location make it a great choice for those who prefer a more personal stay. For more information and reservations, visit myfriendshostel.com.

Academy Hostel: Situated in the San Lorenzo district, Academy Hostel is a well-loved budget accommodation option for those visiting Florence. The hostel offers a range of options from shared dormitories to private rooms, with prices beginning at €25 per night for a bed in a shared dorm and €60 for a private room. Academy Hostel is famous for its central location, just a short walk from Florence's main attractions like the Florence Cathedral, the Medici Chapels, and the Accademia Gallery, where Michelangelo's David is housed. The hostel offers free Wi-Fi, a communal kitchen, and a cozy lounge area with books and board games. Guests can also enjoy a free walking tour of the city, organized by the hostel staff, who are known for their warm and knowledgeable hospitality. A simple breakfast is included in the price of the room, and the hostel also offers discounts for local museums and tours. For reservations and additional information, visit academyhostel.com.

2.3 Boutique Hotels and Luxury Resorts
Florence offers a diverse range of options that cater to the tastes of the most discerning travelers. These exclusive properties combine the best of Tuscan hospitality, world-class amenities, and personalized services, ensuring that every guest's experience is nothing short of extraordinary. Here are exceptional boutique hotels and luxury resorts in Florence that promise an unforgettable stay.

Hotel Savoy: The Hotel Savoy is a prime example of understated luxury in the heart of Florence. This five-star hotel combines contemporary design with classic Florentine style, offering guests a seamless blend of comfort and elegance. Its central location makes it an ideal choice for those wishing to explore Florence's rich history, art, and culture, all within walking distance. The hotel boasts a collection of rooms and suites, each meticulously designed with bespoke furnishings, marble bathrooms, and panoramic views of the city.

Amenities include high-speed Wi-Fi, a state-of-the-art fitness center, and a spa offering rejuvenating treatments. Guests can enjoy delicious Italian cuisine at the hotel's Irene restaurant, where the focus is on local, seasonal ingredients. The prices for rooms typically range from €600 to €1,200 per night, depending on the season and room type. For those looking to indulge further, the Hotel Savoy offers personalized concierge services, including private tours of the city's art galleries, exclusive shopping experiences, and a tailored dining experience. The prices for meals at Irene restaurant range from €50 to €100 per person, offering a variety of delectable options. For bookings and more information, visit their official website: Hotel Savoy Florence

The St. Regis Florence: The St. Regis Florence is the epitome of opulence, offering guests a truly luxurious experience. Housed in a stunning 18th-century palace along the Arno River, this hotel is a masterpiece of classical architecture, with intricately designed frescoes, grand chandeliers, and a rich color palette that evokes a sense of regal splendor. Its strategic location near the Ponte Vecchio and Uffizi Gallery places it at the heart of Florence's artistic and cultural heritage. The hotel's rooms and suites are spacious, featuring luxurious furnishings, marble bathrooms, and breathtaking views of the river or the city. Guests can expect the finest amenities, such as plush bedding, high-tech entertainment systems, and impeccable service. The St. Regis Florence also offers a range of exceptional dining options, including the Michelin-starred Winter Garden by Caino, where guests can enjoy exquisite Italian and Mediterranean dishes. Meal prices at the Winter Garden typically range from €100 to €200 per person. Prices for a night at The St. Regis Florence start at around €700 and can reach €2,500 for its most exclusive suites. Special services include private boat tours along the Arno River, personal shopping assistants, and bespoke spa treatments. The hotel's butler service is also renowned for its attention to detail, ensuring that every guest's need is met with utmost care. For reservations and further details, visit: The St. Regis Florence

Portrait Firenze: For those seeking a more intimate and personalized experience, Portrait Firenze offers an exquisite boutique hotel stay. Located along the Arno River, just steps from the Ponte Vecchio, Portrait Firenze is the epitome of stylish design and sophisticated service. The hotel's contemporary decor is infused with elements of traditional Florentine craftsmanship, creating a sense of warmth and luxury that makes guests feel at home. Each of the hotel's suites is a haven of elegance, complete with private terraces, marble bathrooms, and panoramic views of the Florence skyline. The rooms are designed with attention to detail, blending modern comforts with classic Italian artistry. Prices range from €900 to €2,000 per night, depending on the room category and season. The hotel's in-house restaurant, the Caffè dell'Oro, offers a refined dining experience overlooking the river. The menu showcases a creative take on Tuscan cuisine, with prices typically ranging from €70 to €120 per person. Guests can also enjoy a range of exclusive services, including private shopping tours in the nearby fashion district, wine tasting sessions, and customized excursions to Florence's lesser-known gems. The hotel's concierge team is dedicated to curating unique experiences tailored to each guest's interests. For bookings and more information, visit: Portrait Firenze

Four Seasons Hotel Firenze: The Four Seasons Hotel Firenze is a true sanctuary, offering an experience that blends history with modern luxury. Set within a former convent and surrounded by a lush 11-acre garden, this hotel is an oasis of tranquility amidst the hustle and bustle of Florence. Located near the famous San Lorenzo market and the Accademia Gallery, the hotel offers both privacy and accessibility, making it ideal for travelers looking to explore the city's cultural treasures while enjoying a serene retreat. The Four Seasons features rooms and suites that are both opulent and comfortable, with period furnishings, large windows, and views of the hotel's private gardens or Florence's skyline. The property is renowned for its world-class amenities, including a full-service spa, an outdoor pool, and a fitness center. Room prices generally start at €800 per night and can reach up to €3,500 for the most luxurious suites. For dining, the Four Seasons offers a range of gourmet options, including the Michelin-starred Il Palagio restaurant, where guests can savor refined Italian dishes prepared with the finest local ingredients. Meal prices at Il Palagio typically range from €100 to €200 per person. Guests also have access to personalized services such as private art tours, cooking classes, and helicopter rides over Tuscany. For reservations and more details, visit: Four Seasons Hotel Firenze

Villa Cora: Situated on a hilltop overlooking Florence, Villa Cora is an enchanting luxury resort that combines the charm of a historic villa with the amenities of a modern five-star hotel. This villa dates back to the 19th century and is surrounded by beautiful gardens, offering guests a peaceful retreat from the city's bustle. Located just a short drive from the historic center of Florence, Villa Cora offers both seclusion and convenience for those wanting to explore the city's artistic and cultural riches. The hotel's rooms and suites are spacious and opulent, featuring antique furnishings, marble bathrooms, and private balconies that offer sweeping views of Florence and the Tuscan hills. Prices for rooms start at around €600 per night, with the most exclusive suites priced at €2,000 or more per night. Villa Cora's facilities include a luxurious spa, a heated outdoor pool, and a fully equipped fitness center. The hotel also features a restaurant that serves gourmet Tuscan cuisine, with prices ranging from €50 to €120 per person. Special services include private wine tastings, bespoke cooking classes, and exclusive tours of the Florence countryside. Guests can also enjoy a variety of wellness treatments and massages designed to rejuvenate both body and mind. For bookings and additional information, visit: Villa Cora

2.4 Apartment Rentals and Vacation Homes
Florence offers a variety of lodging options, ranging from luxury hotels to cozy vacation homes and stylish apartment rentals. These rentals provide the perfect balance between comfort, privacy, and the unique charm of living like a local in this remarkable city. In this essay, we will explore distinct apartment rentals and vacation homes, each offering a different experience, complete with detailed information about their locations, prices, amenities, and special services.

La Casa dei Tintori: La Casa dei Tintori offers an authentic and welcoming stay for travelers who wish to immerse themselves in the local culture. Located just steps from the iconic Ponte Vecchio and the Uffizi Gallery, this charming apartment combines the character of old-world Florence with modern comforts. Its spacious interiors are thoughtfully designed with traditional Tuscan touches, such as terracotta floors, wooden beams, and antique furniture. The apartment features one bedroom, a living room, a fully equipped kitchen, and a bathroom with a luxurious marble shower. The price for a one-week stay at La Casa dei Tintori ranges from €1,200 to €1,600, depending on the season, with lower rates in the off-season. Guests enjoy a fully stocked kitchen, free Wi-Fi, air conditioning, and a welcome basket filled with local delicacies such as olive oil and wine. Special services include daily cleaning and concierge assistance, with the option for private tours of Florence's best-hidden gems. For those interested in culinary experiences, the hosts offer private cooking classes where guests can learn how to prepare classic Florentine dishes. For more details or to book a stay, visit their official website at www.lacasadeitintori.com.

The Florentine Loft: For those seeking a blend of contemporary style and classic Florence charm, The Florentine Loft is the ideal choice. Situated in the San Lorenzo district, this sleek and spacious apartment is a short walk from major landmarks such as the Florence Cathedral and the Accademia Gallery, home to Michelangelo's David. With its open-concept design, floor-to-ceiling windows, and minimalist décor, the Florentine Loft appeals to travelers who appreciate modern luxury in the midst of an ancient city. The rental price for The Florentine Loft typically ranges from €1,500 to €2,000 per week, with higher rates during the peak summer months. The apartment features a fully equipped kitchen with high-end appliances, a comfortable living area, two spacious bedrooms, and a private balcony with stunning views of the city skyline. Guests also have access to amenities such as a washer and dryer, high-speed internet, air conditioning, and a smart TV. The hosts provide personalized services, including guided tours, airport transfers, and reservations at Florence's finest restaurants. For more information or to book your stay, visit www.theflorentineloft.com.

Palazzo del Corso: For those seeking a truly luxurious stay, Palazzo del Corso offers an opulent vacation home experience. Located in the heart of the historic city center, this stunning residence occupies a beautifully restored 16th-century building. The grand entrance leads to a spacious living area adorned with antique furnishings, crystal chandeliers, and stunning frescoed ceilings. The apartment offers three lavish bedrooms, each with its own en-suite bathroom, making it perfect for families or groups of friends who value both style and comfort. Prices for a week at Palazzo del Corso start at around €3,500 and can reach up to €5,000 depending on the season. The home includes an array of luxurious amenities, such as a private chef for in-house dining, a dedicated concierge service to assist with any needs, and daily housekeeping. For those looking for a more indulgent experience, a private chauffeur and limousine service are available for sightseeing tours or airport transfers. The property also boasts a beautiful terrace overlooking the city, perfect for enjoying a glass of wine after a day of exploring Florence. To learn more about this exceptional property or to make a reservation, visit www.palazzodelcorso.com.

Residence Hilda: Located in the Oltrarno district, known for its artisan workshops and lively piazzas, Residence Hilda offers a contemporary retreat in one of Florence's most vibrant neighborhoods. This stylish apartment complex consists of several modern, fully furnished apartments that cater to both short-term visitors and long-term stays. The apartments feature sleek interiors with clean lines, high-end finishes, and fully equipped kitchens, offering a perfect blend of modern comfort and Tuscan flair. Residence Hilda is an excellent choice for those who wish to experience Florence from a local's perspective, with attractions like the Pitti Palace and the Boboli Gardens just a short walk away. The price for a one-week stay at Residence Hilda starts at €1,200, with prices varying depending on the apartment size and time of year. The apartments are equipped with amenities such as free Wi-Fi, air conditioning, flat-screen TVs, and kitchen appliances. Residence Hilda also offers additional services like private guided tours, access to a local fitness center, and a bicycle rental program. The property's central location makes it easy to explore Florence on foot, and the nearby artisan shops and cafes add to the neighborhood's charm. For booking or further details, visit their official website at www.residencehilda.com.

Villa La Vedetta: For those seeking a more secluded, tranquil experience, Villa La Vedetta provides a stunning retreat perched on a hilltop overlooking the entire city of Florence. This historic villa, once a private residence, has been meticulously restored to offer a luxurious vacation home experience while maintaining its old-world charm. The villa features elegant interiors with period furnishings, frescoed ceilings, and a beautifully landscaped garden that offers spectacular views of the Tuscan countryside. Prices for a stay at Villa La Vedetta start at €4,000 per week, with the cost rising during peak season. The villa has five spacious bedrooms, each with its own en-suite bathroom, making it ideal for larger families or groups. Guests can enjoy a wide range of amenities, including a private pool, a fully equipped kitchen, air conditioning, and high-speed internet. Special services at Villa La Vedetta include a private chef, daily housekeeping, and personalized tour arrangements. The property also offers a shuttle service to the city center for those who prefer not to drive. To book your stay at this exceptional property or learn more, visit www.villalavedetta.com.

2.5 Unique Accommodations: Villas and Castles

Among the most exclusive and memorable stays are the villas and castles that dot the Tuscan landscape, offering visitors a chance to immerse themselves in the opulence and charm of centuries-old estates. Whether you seek a lavish villa nestled in the hills surrounding Florence or a grandiose castle steeped in history, these accommodations provide a magical blend of tradition, elegance, and comfort. Below are remarkable properties that promise to elevate any visit to Florence, each offering its own distinctive allure, luxurious amenities, and a taste of authentic Italian living.

Villa Cora: Villa Cora, a magnificent 19th-century mansion, stands as a symbol of grandeur just a short distance from the center of Florence. Located on the scenic hillsides of the city, this luxurious villa offers breathtaking views of the surrounding Tuscan countryside. Once a private residence for aristocrats, it has now been transformed into an exquisite five-star hotel. The villa's opulent design features a blend of classic Italian elegance with modern comforts, with rooms decorated in period furniture and tapestries, alongside contemporary amenities like spa services, an outdoor pool, and a well-stocked wine cellar. Prices for lodging at Villa Cora start around €350 per night for a standard room, though suites and special offers may reach up to €1,500 or more per night, depending on the season and room selection. The villa's restaurant is a highlight for guests, offering gourmet Italian cuisine with a focus on local ingredients and traditional recipes. Expect to pay around €50–€80 for a three-course meal, while the wine list features an impressive selection of fine Tuscan wines. Villa Cora also provides exclusive services such as private guided tours, wine tastings, and even personalized spa treatments. Guests can also enjoy access to the wellness center, which includes a sauna, Turkish bath, and massage rooms, offering a truly rejuvenating experience after a day exploring Florence. For more information and bookings, visit their official website at www.villacora.it.

Castello di Vincigliata: For those seeking a fairytale experience, Castello di Vincigliata, located just outside the city, offers an idyllic escape into the past. This medieval castle, perched atop a hill, dates back to the 13th century and provides guests with the rare opportunity to stay within the walls of a historic fortress. The castle offers an array of luxury rooms, each uniquely decorated with antiques and providing stunning views of the Tuscan hills. Prices at Castello di Vincigliata start at approximately €400 per night for a standard double room, while more spacious suites and castle apartments can cost up to

€1,200 per night. The castle also boasts a large garden, perfect for strolling or enjoying a drink in the warm Tuscan sun. Guests can dine at the castle's restaurant, which serves traditional Italian cuisine with a contemporary twist, including classic Tuscan specialties. Expect to pay between €60 and €100 for a meal. The venue also provides specialized services such as private events, weddings, and exclusive tours of the castle and its surroundings. Castello di Vincigliata offers a truly immersive experience in Tuscany's medieval past, making it an ideal destination for those seeking an unforgettable stay in Florence. Visit their website at www.castellodivincigliata.com for bookings and more details.

Villa le Fontanelle: Villa le Fontanelle is a luxury retreat that combines the charm of a Tuscan villa with the elegance of modern amenities. This boutique hotel, once a private villa, has been meticulously restored to retain its historical beauty while offering the comfort and services expected of a five-star property. The villa's rooms are stylishly furnished, blending classic Italian design with contemporary touches, and many feature panoramic views of the city and surrounding vineyards. Rooms start at approximately €300 per night, with suites and specialty rooms available for upwards of €600 per night, depending on the season. Villa le Fontanelle offers a range of high-end amenities, including a wellness center with a heated pool, sauna, and Turkish bath, perfect for guests seeking relaxation after a day exploring Florence. The villa's restaurant serves traditional Tuscan cuisine, with a focus on locally sourced ingredients, offering an unforgettable dining experience for guests. Prices for a meal at the restaurant generally range between €50 and €70 per person for a three-course meal. Additionally, the property provides guests with opportunities for wine tours, cooking classes, and private sightseeing excursions to ensure a memorable and personalized visit. For more information, visit their official website at www.villalefontanelle.com.

Il Salviatino: Il Salviatino, a stunning Renaissance villa located just a few kilometers from Florence's city center, offers a perfect combination of traditional elegance and modern luxury. Set amidst 12 acres of lush gardens and olive groves, the villa boasts panoramic views of the city and the surrounding Tuscan landscape. The rooms and suites are exquisitely decorated with a mix of antique furnishings and modern amenities, including marble bathrooms, plush bedding, and state-of-the-art technology. Prices for a stay at Il Salviatino start around €400 per night for a standard room, with suites ranging up to €1,500 per night during high season. Guests at Il Salviatino can indulge in a range of services, from bespoke spa treatments to private wine tastings. The villa's restaurant, La Terrazza, offers an outstanding culinary experience, serving a range of dishes inspired by traditional Italian cuisine with a contemporary twist. A three-course meal typically costs between €50 and €80. Il Salviatino also offers a variety of specialized services, such as helicopter tours, private art tours of Florence, and tailored excursions throughout Tuscany. To book your stay and learn more, visit www.ilsalviatino.com.

Villa San Michele: Located in the hills above Florence, Villa San Michele is an exclusive luxury hotel that promises a stay like no other. Housed in a former 15th-century monastery, the villa offers sweeping views of the city and the Arno River. The property's design reflects its monastic past, with rooms and suites that feature exposed stone walls, vaulted ceilings, and terracotta floors, combined with contemporary touches for ultimate comfort. Rates at Villa San Michele start at approximately €500 per night for a standard room, with suites ranging up to €1,500 per night. The hotel's Michelin-starred restaurant, La Loggia, offers a fine dining experience that combines Italian classics with creative modern influences. Prices for a meal range from €60 to €120 per person, depending on the course selection. Villa San Michele also provides an array of exclusive services, such as private guided tours, cooking classes, and bespoke experiences tailored to guests' interests. For guests seeking a serene retreat, the villa's spa and wellness center offer a range of treatments and therapies designed to relax and rejuvenate. For more information and reservations, visit their official website at www.villasanmichele.com.

CHAPTER 3
TRANSPORTATION IN FLORENCE

3.1 Getting to Florence

Getting to this cultural gem is a journey of its own, offering diverse and scenic options by air, train, or road. Whether you are traveling from within Italy, Europe, or across the globe, Florence is well-connected and welcoming. Here's an extensive guide to navigating your way to this iconic destination.

Arriving in Florence by Air Travel: For international and long-distance travelers, air travel is often the most convenient way to reach Florence. The city is served by Florence Airport, Peretola (Aeroporto di Firenze-Peretola), officially named Amerigo Vespucci Airport, which lies just 4 kilometers northwest of the city center. While relatively small, this airport is highly efficient and well-connected, especially to European cities. If you're flying from outside Europe, you might first land at major international hubs such as Rome's Leonardo da Vinci Airport (Fiumicino), Milan Malpensa, or even Bologna Airport before connecting to Florence. Airlines like Lufthansa, British Airways, KLM, and Air France frequently operate flights to Florence. Budget carriers, including Ryanair and EasyJet, may use nearby airports like Pisa International Airport (Galileo Galilei), which is just an hour away by train or bus. Ticket prices vary significantly depending on your location, time of booking, and travel season. A one-way ticket from London, for example, can cost as low as €50 with budget airlines if booked in advance, while intercontinental flights from New York might range from €400 to €700. Booking through official airline websites such as www.britishairways.com, www.ryanair.com, or travel aggregators like www.skyscanner.com can help secure the best deals. Consider setting alerts on these platforms for price drops or promotions. Once you land at Florence Airport, getting to the city center is simple. The T2 tram line offers a direct route to the main train station, Santa Maria Novella, in just 20 minutes, costing around €1.50. Alternatively, taxis and shuttle services are readily available.

Traveling to Florence by Train: Italy's rail network is renowned for its efficiency, and Florence stands as a central hub in the system. High-speed trains operated by Trenitalia and Italo provide a swift and comfortable way to arrive in Florence. The city's main station, Firenze Santa Maria Novella (SMN), is located in the heart of the city, just a stone's throw from major landmarks like the Duomo and Ponte Vecchio. For visitors traveling from Rome, the high-speed

Frecciarossa trains make the journey in about 1.5 hours, with ticket prices ranging from €20 to €80, depending on the class and booking time. From Milan, the travel time is around 2 hours, while from Venice, it's about 2.5 hours. Travelers from neighboring European countries can also take advantage of overnight or scenic trains that connect Florence with Paris, Munich, or Zurich. Tickets can be booked online through www.trenitalia.com or www.italotreno.it, and early bookings often come with significant discounts. Most trains offer first and second-class seating, with first class providing more spacious seats and complimentary refreshments. For a luxurious experience, consider booking a business-class or executive-class ticket on the Frecciarossa. Arriving by train allows you to step directly into the pulse of Florence without the hassle of navigating airports or long transfers. The SMN station itself is well-equipped with cafes, luggage storage, and easy access to taxis or local buses.

Reaching Florence by Road: For those who prefer a road trip, driving to Florence offers the chance to experience Tuscany's enchanting countryside. Whether you're arriving from another Italian city or crossing borders from nearby countries like France or Switzerland, the journey promises stunning vistas of rolling hills, vineyards, and charming villages. Florence is accessible via Italy's extensive autostrada (highway) network. The A1 motorway, also known as Autostrada del Sole, connects Florence with major cities like Rome (3 hours) and Milan (4 hours). If you're coming from Pisa or the coast, the A11 motorway will lead you directly to Florence. Car rentals are widely available at airports and city centers across Italy. Companies like Europcar, Hertz, and Avis operate in Florence, offering vehicles at daily rates starting from €40, depending on the model and season. Booking in advance through their websites, such as www.europcar.com or www.hertz.com, often ensures better rates. Keep in mind that Florence's historic center is a ZTL (Zona a Traffico Limitato), where vehicle access is restricted. If you plan to drive, park in designated areas outside the ZTL and explore the city on foot or by public transport. Secure parking facilities are available near the city center, with daily rates averaging €25. For those who prefer not to drive, buses operated by FlixBus and other regional providers connect Florence to numerous cities in Italy and beyond. Tickets can be purchased online at www.flixbus.com for as little as €10 for shorter routes. While bus travel may take longer than trains, it can be a more affordable option for budget-conscious travelers.

3.2 Public Transport: Bus and Train

Florence offers a reliable and efficient way to explore not just the city's treasures but also its surrounding areas. From buses and trams to taxis and rental bicycles, Florence has a variety of public transportation options that cater to both locals and tourists. Understanding these systems is key to navigating the city with ease and experiencing its beauty without unnecessary stress.

The Bus Network: The bus system in Florence is operated by Autolinee Toscane, the main transportation company serving the city and its surrounding regions. Buses are the most commonly used mode of public transport, connecting Florence's major landmarks, neighborhoods, and suburban areas. The network is extensive, and its routes are designed to ensure accessibility to both popular tourist spots and lesser-known corners of the city. A single bus ticket costs €1.50 when purchased in advance from authorized vendors, such as tobacco shops, newsstands, or automated machines. Tickets must be validated upon boarding and are valid for 90 minutes from the time of validation. For those planning to make multiple trips, purchasing a day pass for €5 or a three-day pass for €12 is a cost-effective option. These passes allow unlimited rides within their validity period, making them ideal for visitors aiming to see as much of Florence as possible in a short time. Buses generally run from 5:30 AM to 12:30 AM, with reduced services during nighttime hours. For night owls, the Nottetempo Night Bus service is available on select routes, ensuring that Florence remains navigable even after sunset. While buses can be crowded during peak hours, they remain a dependable choice for getting around.

The Florence Tramway: Florence's tram system is a modern addition to the city's transportation network, offering an efficient way to navigate key areas. Currently, the tramway consists of two main lines: Line T1, which connects Villa Costanza in Scandicci to Careggi Hospital, and Line T2, which links Florence's Peretola Airport to the city center. The tram is particularly appealing to visitors due to its speed and convenience. Trams arrive every 4 to 10 minutes during peak hours and slightly less frequently during off-peak times. Tickets for the tram cost the same as bus tickets—€1.50 for a single ride, with the same options for day or multi-day passes. Tickets can be purchased at tram stops using automated machines and must be validated upon boarding. The tram system is especially useful for travelers arriving at Peretola Airport, as Line T2 provides a direct and inexpensive link to the heart of Florence in approximately

20 minutes. With its clean, spacious carriages and punctual service, the tram is a favorite among both tourists and locals.

Taxis: For those who prioritize convenience, taxis are readily available throughout Florence. Unlike in some cities, hailing a taxi from the street is uncommon in Florence. Instead, taxis must be called via phone or picked up at designated taxi stands, which are typically located near major landmarks, train stations, and squares. Taxis operate on a metered system, with fares starting at around €3.30 during daytime hours and higher at night or on holidays. Additional charges apply for luggage, trips to or from the airport, and advance bookings. While taxis are more expensive than buses or trams, they are a practical option for reaching destinations not easily accessible by public transportation or for those traveling in a group.

Bicycle Rentals and Bike-Sharing Services: For visitors who prefer an active and eco-friendly way to explore Florence, bicycles are an excellent option. The city has embraced cycling as a sustainable mode of transport, with dedicated bike lanes and rental services widely available. Companies like Ridemovi and Florence by Bike offer both short-term and long-term rentals, with prices starting at €10 per day. Bike-sharing services are another popular choice. With the use of a mobile app, visitors can locate and unlock bikes stationed throughout the city. These services charge on a per-minute or per-hour basis, making them a flexible option for short trips or leisurely rides along the Arno River.

Navigating Florence with Public Transportation Apps: To make the most of Florence's public transportation, visitors are encouraged to use mobile apps designed to streamline navigation. Apps like Moovit and Google Maps provide real-time updates on bus and tram schedules, route planning, and walking directions to the nearest stops. These tools are invaluable for tourists unfamiliar with the city's layout, ensuring that they can move around with confidence. Additionally, the Autolinee Toscane app allows users to purchase tickets, view schedules, and access route maps directly from their smartphones. Having these digital tools at hand minimizes the challenges of navigating Florence's transportation network and maximizes the efficiency of every trip.

Practical Tips for Using Public Transportation in Florence: To navigate Florence's public transportation effectively, visitors should plan their routes in advance and familiarize themselves with ticketing procedures. Always validate tickets before starting your journey to avoid fines, and keep an eye on schedules, particularly during weekends and holidays when services may be reduced. Florence's transportation system is designed with accessibility in mind, making it possible to reach most attractions without difficulty. From the grandeur of the Duomo to the artistic splendor of the Uffizi Gallery, the city's buses, trams, and alternative options ensure that every corner of Florence is within reach.

3.3 Taxis and Ride-Sharing Services

Florence's public transport system, though excellent, is complemented by a wide range of taxi and ride-hailing services that provide seamless connectivity to the city's attractions, accommodations, and beyond. Understanding how to use these services effectively will make your visit more comfortable and efficient.

Traditional Taxis: Traditional taxis are a staple of transport in Florence and are easily available at various locations throughout the city, including at major attractions, train stations, and airports. Taxis in Florence are regulated, and fares are set by the local authorities, ensuring consistency and fairness. The standard taxi fare from the airport to the city center is typically between €20 and €30, depending on the exact destination and traffic conditions. Florence's taxis are identifiable by their white color and the "TAXI" sign on top, with the city's emblem on the door. You can hail a taxi directly from the street, although it is advisable to wait at designated taxi ranks, especially during peak hours or in areas with heavy foot traffic. Another option is to call for a taxi via phone or use one of the taxi dispatch apps available in the city. For those looking to book a taxi in advance, several services are available. **Taxi Firenze** is a popular choice, offering both phone bookings and an app for more convenient access. They can be contacted via their website, www.taxifirenze.it, or the app, where visitors can schedule a ride and track the taxi's arrival. The city's taxis operate on a meter system, starting with a base fare of approximately €3.30, with additional charges for distance, waiting time, and services like luggage handling.

Ride-Hailing Services: Ride-hailing services have become a popular and efficient way to travel around Florence, especially for those who are familiar with using mobile apps to order their rides. Companies like Uber, Lyft, and local alternatives have established a strong presence in the city, offering tourists flexibility and ease of use with just a few taps on a smartphone.

Uber: Uber is widely used in Florence, offering a variety of ride options, including UberX for everyday rides and Uber Black for a more luxurious experience. The prices for an Uber ride from the city center to places like the Piazzale Michelangelo or Fiesole can range from €10 to €25, depending on the time of day and demand. Surge pricing may apply during peak hours, but Uber's transparent pricing model ensures that you know the cost upfront before confirming the ride. The Uber app is available for both iOS and Android devices, and visitors can easily register with an international credit card to pay for their trips.

Free Now: Another popular ride-hailing service in Florence is Free Now (formerly known as MyTaxi). This service works similarly to Uber, allowing users to book a taxi via the app and pay directly through the platform. Free Now partners with licensed taxi companies in Florence, so passengers are assured of professional service and local expertise. The app also allows for pre-booking rides, tracking vehicles in real time, and rating drivers, which ensures a high level of customer satisfaction. Prices for a ride with Free Now are comparable to traditional taxis, and the app operates in several other European cities, making it a good choice for travelers familiar with it.

It Taxi is another service that operates via an easy-to-use app. Offering both traditional taxis and ride-hailing options, It Taxi allows users to request a ride from licensed drivers throughout Florence. The app provides real-time tracking and an efficient fare estimator, which ensures that travelers can budget their trips accordingly. In general, a ride through It Taxi is priced similarly to other services, with base fares starting at €3.50, and additional charges for distance traveled and time spent in traffic.

Navigating Effectively with Taxi and Ride-Hailing Services: While Florence is a relatively small city and its main attractions are within walking distance of each other, using a taxi or ride-hailing service can save time when navigating the broader city or heading to less accessible locations. One of the most significant benefits of using these services in Florence is the ease with which visitors can move around, especially when they are unfamiliar with local transport systems or have heavy luggage. To make the most of your taxi or ride-hailing experience in Florence, it is essential to be aware of a few key aspects. First, it's important to understand that most taxi and ride-hailing services charge extra for luggage, typically around €1 to €3 per bag, and additional fees may apply for rides during holidays or after midnight. Additionally, the fares for ride-hailing services like

Uber and Free Now may fluctuate based on demand, so it's advisable to check the price estimate in advance if possible. During peak tourist seasons, ride prices can rise, so pre-booking a ride may help you secure a more predictable fare. For visitors arriving at Florence's main train station, Santa Maria Novella (SMN), taxis are readily available outside the station, but they can be in high demand during busy times. Using an app like Uber or Free Now can be a convenient alternative to waiting in long lines for a taxi. Moreover, these apps offer features that allow you to select the type of car and driver you prefer, giving you an additional layer of flexibility when it comes to your ride. Another factor to consider is Florence's limited traffic zones, or ZTL (Zona a Traffico Limitato), which restrict access to certain areas in the city center. While taxis are generally allowed to enter these zones, ride-hailing services may have limitations depending on where they pick you up or drop you off. It's essential to communicate with your driver if you're unsure about the boundaries of these zones to avoid unnecessary delays or fines.

3.4 Cycling in Florence

Whether wandering through cobbled lanes, cycling along the Arno River, or following historical paths, Florence offers a variety of routes designed to showcase its diverse landscapes and iconic landmarks. Navigating the city by foot or bike allows visitors to experience the true essence of Florence, providing a more intimate connection to its treasures.

The Historic Center Walking Tour: One of the most popular walking routes in Florence is the historic city center, which serves as the heart of the city and houses many of its most famous landmarks. This route is perfect for those who want to explore the rich history and art of Florence at a relaxed pace, and it offers a glimpse into the city's past, from its medieval origins to its Renaissance glory. The journey typically starts at the Piazza del Duomo, where visitors are greeted by the magnificent Cathedral of Santa Maria del Fiore (the Duomo). From here, you can walk to the Piazza della Signoria, passing by the Baptistry of St. John and the Giotto Bell Tower, which are stunning examples of Gothic architecture. Continuing along the Via dei Calzaiuoli, you'll find the Palazzo Vecchio, Florence's medieval town hall, before reaching the famous Ponte Vecchio, the city's iconic bridge. From the bridge, it's a short walk to the Uffizi Gallery, home to one of the world's most important collections of Renaissance art. This route is a must for anyone wishing to absorb the essence of Florence, with plenty of cafes and shops where you can pause and take in the vibrant atmosphere. This walking tour is easily navigable and suitable for people of all fitness levels. While the streets can get crowded, particularly during peak tourist seasons, the central pedestrian areas are well-maintained and offer a safe environment for exploration. Visitors can take their time, pausing at any of the numerous historical sites, galleries, and piazzas along the way.

The Arno River Cycle Path: For those who prefer cycling, the Arno River Cycle Path offers a stunning route that takes cyclists along the Arno River, the waterway that has shaped Florence's development throughout history. The cycle path stretches for several kilometers, offering panoramic views of the river and the city skyline, as well as a unique perspective on some of Florence's most iconic landmarks. Starting from the Piazza Santa Croce, this cycling route follows the Arno River eastward, passing under the Ponte Vecchio and providing spectacular views of the Pitti Palace and the Boboli Gardens. As you continue along the river, you can cross over the Ponte San Niccolò and ride through the quieter streets near the San Miniato al Monte hill, where a detour can be made for a visit to this historic church with one of the best panoramic views of the city. The Arno River Cycle Path is generally flat and safe for cyclists, making it an excellent route for beginners and those who want to enjoy Florence's scenic beauty without navigating the busier city streets. Bikes can be rented from various shops in the city, and there are plenty of designated bike lanes along the river, making it a safe and relaxing way to experience the city's charm.

The Boboli Gardens and Forte di Belvedere Circuit: For those seeking a combination of walking and cycling through Florence's green spaces, the Boboli Gardens and Forte di Belvedere Circuit offers a wonderful opportunity to explore the city's historical and natural landscapes. This route combines the elegance of the Renaissance gardens with the historic charm of the Forte di Belvedere, a fortress offering some of the best views of Florence. The journey begins at the Pitti Palace, from where you can enter the Boboli Gardens, a vast green space filled with sculptures, fountains, and hedged paths. As you cycle or walk through the gardens, you will come across several grottos, ornate gardens, and stunning terraces that offer sweeping views over Florence. After exploring the gardens, you can continue up to the Forte di Belvedere, a historical fortress atop a hill. From the fortress, you'll be rewarded with a panoramic view of Florence, with the Duomo rising majestically in the distance.

The Fiesole Hillside Route: For those who wish to experience a more rural side of Florence, the Fiesole Hillside Route offers a scenic cycling escape into the

Tuscan countryside. Starting from the city center, this route takes cyclists on a journey up the hills surrounding Florence, offering breathtaking views of the city and the rolling Tuscan hills. The ride begins at Piazza della Liberta, where cyclists can follow the Via San Domenico to reach Fiesole, a charming town situated on the hills just north of Florence. The route is steep, with some challenging sections, but the reward is the view of Florence from above and the tranquility of the countryside. Fiesole itself is a charming town, home to Roman ruins, an ancient theater, and stunning views over Florence. Visitors can take a break here, enjoy a meal at one of the town's cafes, and explore its archaeological sites before cycling back to the city. This cycling route is more challenging than those within the city limits but offers a unique opportunity to experience the beauty of the Tuscan countryside. It's ideal for experienced cyclists or those looking for a more active adventure. Along the way, cyclists can stop at various viewpoints, making it an ideal route for photography enthusiasts.

The Cascine Park Walk: For those seeking a peaceful and leisurely walking route, the Cascine Park offers a serene escape from the urban environment. As Florence's largest park, it stretches along the western bank of the Arno River and provides ample space for both walking and cycling. The park is ideal for a relaxing stroll, with tree-lined paths, open fields, and tranquil areas to sit and enjoy nature. Visitors can start at the Piazza Vittorio Veneto, which marks the entrance to the park, and meander through its expansive grounds. The park also hosts various historical and cultural landmarks, such as the Villa Demidoff and the Cascine Racetrack, which are worth exploring. The park's paths are well-suited for walking, and there are several cycling routes within the park for those who prefer two wheels. Cascine Park is an excellent choice for visitors seeking a less tourist-heavy route, offering a relaxing atmosphere where one can enjoy nature, local life, and scenic views without the crowds of the historic city center. It's particularly lovely in the spring and summer months, when the park is lush and green.

3.5 Car Rentals and Driving Tips
Whether you're planning to explore the scenic Tuscan countryside or need the flexibility to visit the surrounding areas, car rentals offer the freedom to discover Florence and its beautiful surroundings at your own pace. However, it's important to be aware of driving regulations, parking restrictions, and the best rental companies in the area to make the process smooth and enjoyable.

The Benefits of Renting a Car in Florence: Renting a car in Florence can significantly enhance your experience, especially if you wish to explore beyond the city's historical limits. The surrounding Tuscany region offers an abundance of vineyards, hilltop towns, and picturesque villages that are best accessed by car. With the ability to visit remote locations such as Chianti, San Gimignano, and the Val d'Orcia, a rental car provides convenience and the ability to stop wherever you desire. While Florence itself is compact and easy to walk around, a car gives you the flexibility to venture further afield. Additionally, if you plan on traveling to nearby cities like Siena, Pisa, or Lucca, having a car makes it more convenient and cost-effective compared to relying on public transportation. However, it's crucial to understand that driving in the historical center of Florence is heavily regulated, and tourists are advised to be cautious about where they park and whether they enter the ZTL (Limited Traffic Zone), as driving within this area without proper authorization can result in hefty fines.

Understanding Driving in Florence: Driving in Florence, especially within the city center, can be challenging for those unfamiliar with its narrow streets and heavy traffic. The city's historical core is a maze of cobblestone alleys, one-way streets, and pedestrian zones. Most tourists will find that driving within the historic center is not only unnecessary but also restrictive due to the ZTL zones that limit access to vehicles during certain hours. These areas are enforced with cameras and fines, so it's crucial to stay within the designated traffic routes. When driving outside the historical center, Florence becomes more manageable. The city is well connected by major highways such as the Autostrada del Sole (A1), which allows for quick travel to and from other cities. However, parking can be scarce and expensive in Florence. Many visitors find it more practical to park at one of the several Park **and Ride** facilities located on the outskirts of the city and use public transportation to get to the center.

Rental Car Companies in Florence: For those who decide to rent a car, Florence offers a wide range of reputable rental companies, each offering different types of vehicles and rental terms. These companies are conveniently located in various parts of the city, including at the Amerigo Vespucci Airport and the Santa Maria Novella Train Station, allowing visitors to pick up their vehicles upon arrival.

Europcar: One well-known option is Europcar, located at Via di Novoli, 101 near Amerigo Vespucci Airport. Europcar provides a broad selection of vehicles, from compact cars ideal for navigating Florence's narrow streets to larger models for exploring Tuscany. Their pricing starts at around €40 per day for a basic compact car, but the rates can fluctuate depending on the season and the type of vehicle you choose. You can make reservations directly on their website at www.europcar.com.

Santa Maria Novella Train Station: Another reliable option is **Avis**, which has a location at the Santa Maria Novella Train Station at Piazza della Stazione, 1. Avis is known for its excellent customer service and offers a range of cars suited for city driving as well as long-distance road trips through the countryside. Prices at Avis typically start around €50 per day for a small sedan, with larger vehicles and luxury cars available for higher rates. To reserve a car or check availability, visit www.avis.com.

Hertz is another prominent rental agency with a location at Piazza della Stazione, 1, conveniently near the train station. Hertz is known for offering competitive prices and a diverse fleet that includes both economical vehicles and luxury models. Rental prices for a basic vehicle start at about €45 per day. For more details, reservations, or specific requirements, their website www.hertz.com is a great resource.

Italy by Car: For a more local touch, consider Italy by Car, a company located at Viale Belfiore, 41. Known for providing excellent customer service and a fleet of well-maintained cars, Italy by Car offers both short-term rentals and longer rentals for travelers wishing to explore Tuscany. Their prices are competitive, starting from around €40 per day for a small car. Their website, www.italybycar.it, provides detailed information on available vehicles and booking options.

Sixt is another established name in the car rental industry, with a location at Viale Gramsci, 8, close to the city center. Sixt offers a range of cars from compact models to SUVs and luxury vehicles. Their rates start at around €40 per day, with various options depending on your requirements. Booking can be done via their website at www.sixt.com.

Rental Costs and Booking Tips: When renting a car in Florence, the cost will depend on several factors, including the type of vehicle, the rental duration, and the time of year. Rates tend to be higher during peak travel seasons, such as spring and summer, when tourists flock to the city. It is always a good idea to book your rental car in advance, especially during the high season, to ensure availability and secure the best rates. Most rental companies offer both short-term and long-term rentals, with options ranging from daily to weekly rates. Keep in mind that additional fees may apply, such as insurance coverage, fuel charges, and additional driver fees. Many rental companies provide the option of purchasing insurance coverage, but be sure to review the terms to ensure you're adequately covered. In addition to the rental fee, most agencies will place a deposit on your credit card, which is refunded when the car is returned in good condition. Some companies may also offer extras such as GPS devices, car seats, or additional insurance for an extra charge.

Picking Up and Returning the Car: Rental car pickup and return procedures are straightforward in Florence, especially if you're picking up your car at Florence Airport or Santa Maria Novella Train Station. For those arriving by air, you can easily access the car rental desks directly in the airport terminal. In the city, rental agencies are often located near major transportation hubs, making it easy to collect and drop off the car. It's important to be aware of Florence's ZTL (Limited Traffic Zones), which restrict access to many central areas of the city. When driving in Florence, make sure you understand where these zones are and avoid entering them without authorization. Most car rental companies will provide clear guidelines to help you avoid fines. Additionally, when returning the vehicle, it's advisable to park it at a designated rental parking lot near the agency's office.

3.6 Parking and Traffic Information

Florence is an enchanting city to visit. However, its popularity as a tourist destination comes with challenges for visitors driving into the city, particularly regarding parking and navigating the city's sometimes complex traffic regulations. With limited space in the historic center and the prevalence of pedestrian-only zones, understanding parking options and the traffic rules is essential for a smooth experience. Visitors planning to drive or rent a car in Florence must be prepared for the city's traffic conditions, which can be quite different from other cities. The following is a comprehensive overview of parking options and traffic information in Florence that every visitor should know.

Parking in the Historic Center: The historic center of Florence, which is also a UNESCO World Heritage site, is characterized by its narrow streets and a large number of attractions packed closely together. As a result, parking in the center is extremely limited and often not the most convenient option for tourists. The city has designated a **Zona a Traffico Limitato** (ZTL), or Limited Traffic Zone, in the central areas to reduce congestion, protect its historical structures, and encourage alternative modes of transportation. Driving into this zone without proper authorization is not only inconvenient but also costly, as fines can be issued. The ZTL operates from Monday to Friday, with different hours for weekdays and weekends. Vehicles entering this zone without the proper permissions are subject to hefty fines, and signs around the zone indicate where the restrictions apply. Visitors with hotel bookings within the ZTL may be able to request temporary access permits from their accommodation, allowing them to enter the area to unload luggage or check in. However, access is strictly regulated, and only residents or authorized vehicles are allowed within the ZTL during operational hours. Given the limited parking options within the ZTL and the associated fines, visitors are encouraged to park outside the historic center and use public transport or walk to reach the attractions. This allows visitors to enjoy Florence without the stress of navigating its congested streets.

Public Parking Garages and Areas Around the City: Outside the ZTL zone, there are several public parking garages and parking areas where visitors can leave their cars safely. The most convenient of these are usually located at the entrances to the historic center, where visitors can easily access the major tourist sites either on foot or by public transport. Parking garages near Piazzale Michelangelo offer a scenic and accessible location with fantastic views of the city. From here, it's easy to walk down to the city center, where many of Florence's key attractions, including the Piazza del Duomo and the Ponte Vecchio, are located. Another popular parking option is Parcheggio Santa Maria Novella, located near the central train station. This garage is well-placed for those arriving by train but wishing to drive into the city afterward. It's an excellent option for visitors who need access to both the train station and the city center. Other parking areas can be found at locations like Parcheggio Stazione Firenze Rifredi or Parcheggio Porta Romana, both offering affordable rates and relatively easy access to Florence's main attractions. For those seeking even more affordable options, on-street parking in Florence is available, but it is rare and often restricted to certain hours. The on-street parking spaces are divided into zones marked by blue lines. These spots require payment via a parking meter or mobile app, and the rates vary depending on the area. Be aware that these spaces can be limited and are often filled quickly, especially during peak tourist seasons.

Traffic Rules and Navigation: Driving in Florence, especially in the historic center, requires careful attention to traffic rules and regulations. One of the most important aspects of navigating the city is understanding the **ZTL** zones, as discussed earlier. Failing to comply with these regulations can result in significant fines, so visitors should always be aware of their surroundings and the designated traffic restrictions. In addition to ZTL zones, Florence has other important traffic regulations that visitors should keep in mind. One of the challenges of driving in Florence is the lack of traditional street signs. In the historic center, many streets are quite narrow, and one-way systems are in place, which may not always be obvious to first-time visitors. It is also common to encounter pedestrians and cyclists, so drivers must remain vigilant at all times. Parking in the city is also difficult due to the limited availability of spots, particularly near major tourist attractions. This makes it advisable for visitors to park in a garage or designated lot and use public transportation or walk to the attractions instead of trying to navigate the busy city streets. Florence's streets can get congested, especially during the high tourist season, so patience is key. Public transportation, including buses, trams, and taxis, is a more efficient alternative for visitors wishing to avoid the frustrations of city traffic. Most visitors find that using a combination of public transport and walking allows them to enjoy Florence's beauty without the stress of navigating the city's streets.

Tips for Efficient Navigation in Florence: For those determined to drive into the city center, there are a few tips that can help ensure a smoother experience. First, visitors should familiarize themselves with Florence's road network and be mindful of the ZTL zones, which are clearly marked with signs in both Italian and English. It is also recommended to use a GPS or navigation app to help with directions, as this can provide real-time information on traffic conditions and help avoid restricted areas. If you are staying at a hotel in the city center, check whether the hotel offers parking facilities or permits for ZTL access. Many hotels provide discounted rates for parking in nearby garages, and some even offer parking packages that include access to the ZTL for a limited time. For those visiting for a day, using P+R (Park and Ride) options is an excellent way to avoid the hassle of driving into the heart of the city. Parking lots located on the outskirts of Florence are connected to the city center via public transport or shuttles, allowing visitors to park their car safely and travel easily into the historic center. It's also worth noting that Florence has an efficient public transport system, with buses, trams, and taxis providing excellent connectivity.

CHAPTER 4
TOP 10 MUST-SEE ATTRACTIONS

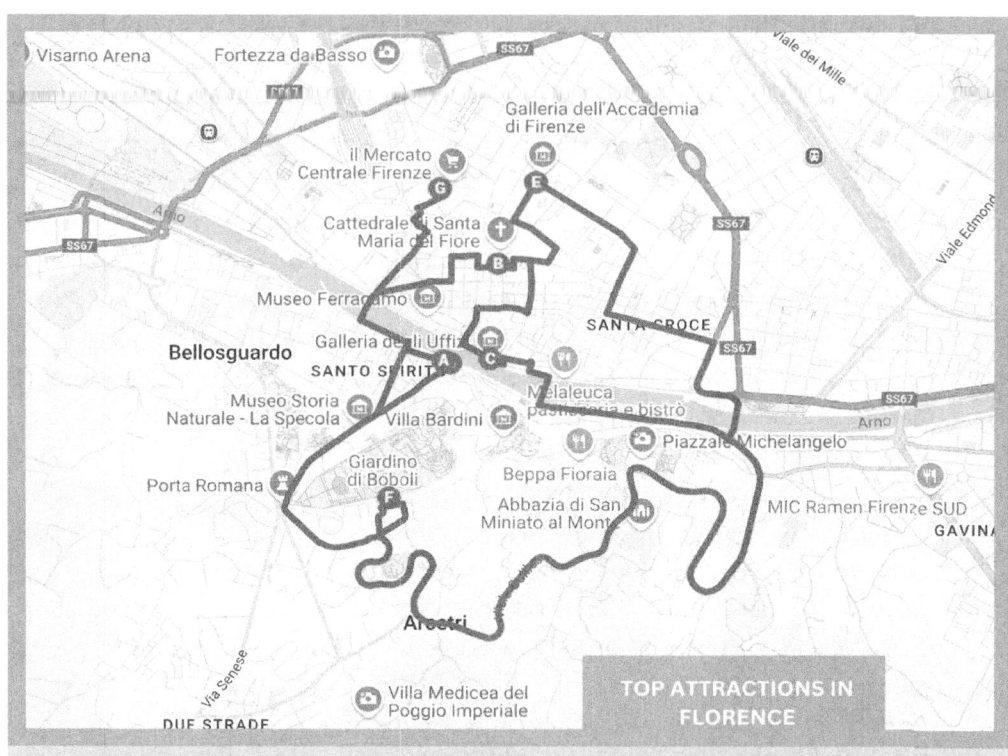

TOP ATTRACTIONS IN FLORENCE

Directions from Florence, Italy to Piazzale Michelangelo, Piazzale Michelangelo, Florence, Metropolitan City of Florence, Italy

A
Florence, Italy

B
Cathedral of Santa Maria del Fiore, Piazza del Duomo, Florence, Metropolitan City of Florence, Italy

C
Uffizi Gallery, Piazzale degli Uffizi, Florence, Metropolitan City of Florence, Italy

D
Ponte Vecchio, Ponte Vecchio, Florence, Metropolitan City of Florence, Italy

E
Accademia Gallery, Via Ricasoli, Florence, Metropolitan City of Florence, Italy

F
Giardino di Boboli, Florence, Metropolitan City of Florence, Italy

G
il Mercato Centrale Firenze, Via dell'Ariento, Florence, Metropolitan City of Florence, Italy

H
Santa Croce, Basilica di Santa Croce, Piazza di Santa Croce, Florence, Metropolitan City of Florence, Italy

I
Piazzale Michelangelo, Piazzale Michelangelo, Florence, Metropolitan City of Florence, Italy

47

4.1 Cathedral of Santa Maria del Fiore (Duomo)

The Cathedral of Santa Maria del Fiore, more commonly known as the Duomo, stands as the heart of Florence, a stunning testament to the city's artistic and architectural mastery. Whether you're a history enthusiast, a lover of art, or simply seeking to immerse yourself in the grandeur of Florence, the Duomo offers a wealth of experiences that will leave you spellbound. Here are must-see places within the Duomo complex that are sure to captivate your senses and ignite your curiosity.

The Dome of Brunelleschi: The most iconic feature of the Duomo is undoubtedly the magnificent dome designed by Filippo Brunelleschi. For centuries, it stood as an engineering wonder, challenging the boundaries of architecture and construction. Climbing the 463 steps to the top is no easy feat, but the effort is rewarded with a breathtaking view of Florence that seems to stretch on endlessly. From here, you can gaze down upon the terracotta rooftops, the winding Arno River, and the entire Tuscan countryside. Standing on the dome, surrounded by the vast sky and the distant hills, you'll understand why this architectural feat remains an awe-inspiring symbol of human ingenuity.

The Baptistery of St. John: Just steps away from the Duomo, the Baptistery of St. John beckons visitors with its timeless beauty. Dating back to the 11th century, this octagonal structure is one of the oldest buildings in Florence. Inside, you'll encounter some of the most exquisite mosaics ever created, particularly the striking golden dome that depicts the Last Judgment. The

Baptistery's intricate marble floors and the celebrated Gates of Paradise by Lorenzo Ghiberti make it an essential part of the Duomo experience. As you step into this sacred space, you can't help but feel the weight of centuries of history and devotion that have passed through these walls.

The Cathedral Interior: While the exterior of the Duomo is jaw-dropping, stepping inside the cathedral is like entering a vast, sacred world of artistic brilliance. The soaring columns and ornate details are bathed in light that filters through the stained-glass windows, casting colorful patterns onto the marble floors. The high altar, adorned with magnificent sculptures and religious artwork, is a testament to Florence's devotion to both God and art. One of the most remarkable features is Giorgio Vasari's frescoes in the dome's interior, depicting the Last Judgment. As you stand beneath the massive dome, the vibrant colors and meticulous details invite you to contemplate the divine while marveling at the skill required to create such an immersive masterpiece.

The Museo dell'Opera del Duomo: For those with a deep appreciation for the Duomo's rich artistic heritage, the Museo dell'Opera del Duomo is a must-visit. Situated just behind the cathedral, this museum houses many of the original artworks and sculptures that once adorned the cathedral, baptistery, and bell tower. Here, you can stand face-to-face with Donatello's sculptures, Michelangelo's unfinished "Pietà," and the delicate marble reliefs by Andrea Pisano. The museum is a journey through Florence's artistic evolution, and it offers an intimate view of how the Duomo came to life through the hands of Renaissance masters. Each piece tells a story of devotion, craftsmanship, and artistic brilliance.

Giotto's Campanile: Another gem in the Duomo complex is the Campanile, or bell tower, designed by Giotto. At 82 meters tall, the tower offers an unparalleled panoramic view of the city, rivaling that of Brunelleschi's dome. Though the climb is steep, the sense of achievement when you reach the top is unmatched. The Campanile's delicate stonework and sculptural details are also worth admiring up close. You'll notice how its design complements the grandeur of the Duomo, forming a harmonious architectural ensemble that continues to draw the admiration of visitors from around the world.

4.2 Uffizi Gallery

The Uffizi Gallery in Florence is not just a museum; it's a journey through time, a place where art and history blend in mesmerizing harmony. With each room filled with treasures that span centuries, this gallery offers an unforgettable experience that stirs the soul. Whether you're an art lover or a curious traveler, here are unmissable places to see in the Uffizi that will leave you in awe.

The Birth of Venus by Sandro Botticelli: Stepping into the room where Botticelli's The Birth of Venus hangs is like entering a dream. This masterpiece, with its ethereal beauty, draws you in with the grace and mystery of Venus, emerging from the sea on a shell. The colors are soft yet vivid, the figures almost floating in a divine moment of creation. It's as if time stops, and you're left staring at a scene that transcends both earthly and divine realms. The delicate beauty and symbolism of this painting are more than just visually stunning; they are a testament to human creativity and imagination. You'll find yourself captivated by the way Botticelli captures a moment of transformation—where mythology and beauty converge in a timeless masterpiece.

The Annunciation by Leonardo da Vinci: Leonardo da Vinci's Annunciation is another jewel of the Uffizi that speaks volumes without uttering a word. This early work of Leonardo's showcases the angel Gabriel delivering the news to the Virgin Mary. The interplay of light and shadow, the tender expression on Mary's face, and the detailed landscape in the background all combine to create a scene of profound tranquility. Standing before this painting, you'll feel the serenity and quiet anticipation of the moment. The delicate, almost ethereal quality of the figures, coupled with Leonardo's meticulous attention to detail, will make you pause and reflect. It's a moment frozen in time, a glimpse into the artist's genius that still resonates with us today.

The Adoration of the Magi by Gentile da Fabriano: As you make your way through the gallery, you'll be drawn to The Adoration of the Magi by Gentile da Fabriano, a dazzling display of Gothic art that is rich in color, detail, and symbolism. The scene, depicting the three kings offering their gifts to the infant Jesus, is a spectacle of opulence. The intricate details of the royal garments, the lush landscape, and the exquisite facial expressions of the figures are enough to make you feel like you've stepped into a medieval court. What makes this piece so special is not just its aesthetic beauty but its vivid portrayal of divine and earthly realms coming together. It's an invitation to witness an extraordinary moment in history, painted with a level of refinement that remains unparalleled.

The Tondo Doni by Michelangelo: Michelangelo's Tondo Doni is a stunning example of Renaissance artistry. This circular painting, depicting the Holy Family, stands out not only because of its size but because of the intense emotion it conveys. The figures are rendered in a dynamic, almost sculptural manner, a hallmark of Michelangelo's style. The muscular form of the Virgin Mary, the vivid colors, and the dramatic poses of the figures all convey a sense of movement and life. When you look at this work, you can't help but feel a connection to the figures—there's a humanity and warmth in the way Michelangelo captures this sacred moment. It's as if the figures are about to step out of the painting and into the room with you.

The Madonna of the Goldfinch by Raphael: One of Raphael's finest works, The Madonna of the Goldfinch, captures the tenderness and grace of motherhood in a way that feels both deeply personal and universally resonant. The scene portrays the Virgin Mary with the infant Jesus and John the Baptist, holding a small goldfinch. The serenity in their faces, the soft lighting, and the delicate balance of figures create a sense of harmony that is almost palpable. What makes this painting stand out is not just the beauty of the figures, but the profound simplicity of the scene. It speaks to something deep within—the love and devotion that define human relationships, all captured in a masterful work of art. It's a moment frozen in time, radiating peace and warmth.

4.3 Ponte Vecchio

Florence offers an array of experiences that captivate the soul. Among its most iconic landmarks is the Ponte Vecchio, the old bridge that has stood over the Arno River for centuries. Here are places you can explore nearby that will leave you with unforgettable memories and an irresistible desire to return to Florence.

Piazza della Signoria: Just a short stroll from Ponte Vecchio, Piazza della Signoria serves as Florence's open-air museum. The square is surrounded by some of the most important historical buildings, like the Palazzo Vecchio and the Loggia dei Lanzi, where you can marvel at sculptures like the towering Perseus with the Head of Medusa by Benvenuto Cellini. What truly draws visitors, however, is the square's ability to transport you back in time. Standing in the piazza, surrounded by works of art and architecture, you can feel the pulse of Florence's rich political and cultural history. It's a place that invites reflection, yet fills you with excitement, as you realize that you're standing in the very heart of the city.

Boboli Gardens: Behind the Pitti Palace, which is just a short walk across the Arno from Ponte Vecchio, lies the stunning Boboli Gardens. These beautifully manicured gardens offer more than just a peaceful retreat from the bustling city streets—they are a masterpiece in themselves. As you wander through the lush greenery, past fountains and statues, you'll discover hidden corners and sweeping views of Florence that take your breath away. The gardens offer a perfect blend of nature and art, with a sense of quiet grandeur that encourages deep reflection. Whether you're strolling through the shaded avenues or gazing at the magnificent views from the **Grotta del Buontalenti**, Boboli Gardens provide an oasis of serenity right in the heart of Florence.

Vasari Corridor: An often-overlooked gem, the Vasari Corridor offers a fascinating peek into Florence's rich history. This elevated passageway, which connects the Uffizi Gallery to the Pitti Palace, was originally designed for the ruling Medici family to safely traverse the city without mingling with the public. Today, it is home to an eclectic collection of art, including portraits of the most notable figures of the Renaissance. Walking through the corridor is like entering a secret world—one where history is preserved in its most intimate form. The corridor also offers incredible views of the Ponte Vecchio and the Arno River, making it a must-see for any history or art lover.

Piazza Santo Spirito: While many tourists flock to the more famous squares of Florence, Piazza Santo Spirito offers a more authentic, local experience. Located on the other side of the Arno River, this lively square is surrounded by cafés, restaurants, and artisan shops, and it's a perfect spot to enjoy the Italian way of life. The Basilica di Santo Spirito, designed by Brunelleschi, stands proudly in the center of the piazza, offering a peaceful sanctuary. But the true charm of this square lies in the way it buzzes with life—Florentines of all ages gather here to socialize, enjoy a glass of wine, or simply soak in the atmosphere. It's a place where time slows down, and you'll find yourself savoring every moment of the experience.

4.4 Accademia Gallery

One of the most iconic and awe-inspiring sights in the Accademia Gallery in Florence is Michelangelo's David. Standing at an imposing 17 feet tall, this monumental statue is a testament to human strength, beauty, and artistic genius. When you stand before it, you can't help but be taken aback by the intricacy of its details, from the taut muscles of his body to the almost lifelike expression of determination on his face. The statue, sculpted between 1501 and 1504, was originally meant to adorn the Florence Cathedral, but its majesty demanded a more prominent setting. Now, in the Accademia, it draws visitors from around the world who are eager to witness this timeless representation of the biblical hero. As you approach David, take a moment to appreciate the history and symbolism encapsulated in this remarkable work, for it tells the story of Florence itself—brimming with resilience and beauty.

The Galleria dell'Accademia: As you explore the Accademia Gallery, the surrounding walls showcase a collection of magnificent paintings that represent the progression of art during the Renaissance. Among them, the Prisoners (or Slaves) by Michelangelo stands out. These unfinished sculptures of struggling figures, bound by rough marble, have captivated art lovers for centuries. The tension in their forms, still emerging from the stone, evokes a sense of unfulfilled potential. They hint at the raw process of creation, where even unfinished works convey emotion and grandeur. Standing in front of them, you feel the tension of both the artist's and the subjects' struggles, sparking a deep connection with the human condition. This encounter offers an introspective exploration of how art can express what words cannot.

The Painted Glory of Florentine Renaissance Art: The Galleria dell'Accademia also houses a remarkable collection of Renaissance art, including works by artists like Sandro Botticelli, Domenico Ghirlandaio, and the visionary painter Pietro Perugino. The brightly colored canvases reveal the power of the human form, the divine, and the worldly scenes of life. Botticelli's Madonna and Child with Angels enchants with its ethereal beauty, while Ghirlandaio's Adoration of the Magi transports you to a moment of serene reverence. These works are not just paintings; they are windows into the spirit of Renaissance Florence, inviting you to understand the devotion, beauty, and the ever-evolving understanding of humanity that defined the period. Every brushstroke tells a story of its time, making each gallery room feel like a portal to the past.

The Hall of Musical Instruments: For something truly unique, the Accademia also features a remarkable collection of historical musical instruments. The Museo degli Strumenti Musicali (Museum of Musical Instruments) is a treasure trove of sound and history. Here, you'll find beautifully crafted violins, harpsichords, and early stringed instruments that once echoed in the courtrooms and salons of Renaissance Florence. Each piece tells the story of a different era in the history of music, showing how sound and craftsmanship intersected to create melodies that would echo through history. Imagine the melodies that once filled the air as you stand before these beautiful instruments, now preserved for your admiration. It's an immersive experience that deepens your understanding of the artistic culture of Florence, where visual art and music blended harmoniously.

The Museum's Vibrant Temporary Exhibitions: While the Accademia's permanent collection is world-renowned, it also hosts rotating exhibitions that provide fresh perspectives on art, history, and culture. These exhibitions showcase diverse themes and time periods, often highlighting lesser-known artists or specific art movements. Each new exhibition offers an opportunity to experience the ever-changing landscape of art in Florence. Whether it's a collection of contemporary art, a retrospective of an iconic artist, or an exploration of a unique aspect of Italian history, these exhibits will captivate your imagination and broaden your appreciation of the arts. It's an invitation to return to the gallery time and again, knowing that each visit will offer something new, something unexpected—yet always extraordinary.

4.5 Palazzo Pitti and Boboli Gardens

The Palazzo Pitti and Boboli Gardens stand as symbols of Renaissance grandeur. To visit these sites is to step into the world of powerful rulers, exquisite art collections, and breathtaking landscapes. Here are remarkable places to discover within the majestic Palazzo Pitti and its surrounding gardens, each offering a unique glimpse into the past and an experience that will leave you spellbound.

The Palatine Gallery: The Palatine Gallery within Palazzo Pitti is an unparalleled treasure trove of Renaissance art. As you step inside, the rich history of Florence unfurls before you. This grand museum, located on the piano nobile (noble floor), boasts works by masters such as Raphael, Titian, and Caravaggio. The walls are adorned with masterpieces that tell stories of love, power, and intrigue, and the rooms themselves feel like an extension of the art. Strolling through this collection is like wandering through a dream where the past's most influential figures come to life. The vivid colors, intricate details, and sweeping portraits evoke emotions that transcend time, inviting you to reflect on the magnificence of Florence's artistic legacy.

The Royal Apartments: Walking through the Royal Apartments of the Palazzo Pitti feels like stepping back into the opulent world of Italian nobility. These rooms, once inhabited by the ruling families of Tuscany, reveal the splendor of aristocratic living during the 16th and 17th centuries. The interiors are a spectacle of richly decorated walls, lavish furniture, and intricate tapestries that offer a window into the grandeur of Florentine court life. Each room tells its own story, with a blend of artistry and function that reflects the tastes of the period. The richness of the royal decor, coupled with the historical significance of these rooms, will transport you to an era of elegance and power.

The Boboli Gardens: The Boboli Gardens, located just behind Palazzo Pitti, are a masterpiece of landscape design. This sprawling park is a blend of art, nature, and history, with fountains, sculptures, and manicured pathways leading visitors through its verdant expanse. As you wander through the gardens, you're met with sweeping views of Florence below, framed by cypress trees and classical statues that evoke the grandeur of Renaissance garden design. The Garden of the Cavalier, with its geometric patterns and central fountain, is a particular highlight—its symmetry and beauty echo the ideals of harmony that were central to Renaissance thinking. It's not just a garden; it's an open-air museum that encourages introspection and wonder, offering moments of peace and beauty at every turn.

The Costume Gallery: For something truly unique, the Costume Gallery within the Palazzo Pitti offers an intriguing look at the evolution of fashion through the ages. Housed in the royal palace's former stables, this museum showcases an impressive collection of historic costumes, textiles, and accessories. As you move from room to room, you'll witness the transformation of Italian fashion, from elaborate 16th-century court attire to the more streamlined elegance of the 19th century. The gallery isn't just about clothes; it's a deep dive into the cultural shifts and social changes that influenced what people wore. The delicate fabrics, intricate embroidery, and stunning accessories give a palpable sense of the artistry and craftsmanship that defined each era.

The Amphitheater and Grottos: In the heart of the Boboli Gardens is the enchanting Amphitheater and its series of grottos. While many visitors are drawn to the more famous areas of the gardens, this secluded spot offers an atmosphere of mystery and charm that's often overlooked. The amphitheater, built in the late 16th century, was designed for theatrical performances and is an evocative setting for those who appreciate both history and the arts. Surrounding it are intricately designed grottos—natural-looking caves adorned with shells, stones, and moss—that transport you into another world. The stillness and beauty of this area make it one of the most romantic and serene corners of the gardens, where you can pause and take in the tranquil surroundings.

4.6 San Lorenzo Market

San Lorenzo Market is not just a place to shop—it's a sensory journey that captures the essence of Tuscan life. This bustling market, rich in history and brimming with charm, offers a fascinating blend of local culture, tradition, and artistry. Whether you're a seasoned traveler or a first-time visitor, here are unforgettable experiences to immerse yourself in at this iconic Florentine landmark.

The Historic Market Stalls: As you step into the San Lorenzo Market, you're immediately greeted by a symphony of sights, sounds, and scents. The outdoor stalls, tucked under the shadow of the Basilica di San Lorenzo, offer an array of goods that are a testament to Florence's vibrant artisan culture. From handmade leather bags to intricately designed scarves, these stalls are a treasure trove for unique souvenirs. The raw energy of the vendors, the bright colors of the merchandise, and the tantalizing aromas of fresh produce and cured meats create an atmosphere that is both lively and authentic. Wandering through these stalls, you can't help but feel the pulse of the city—each item, whether it's a handmade piece of jewelry or a vibrant Tuscan ceramic, tells a story of craftsmanship and tradition. As you haggle over a handwoven tablecloth or a bottle of local olive oil, you'll realize that you're not just purchasing a souvenir, but taking home a slice of Florence's soul.

Mercato Centrale: Just a few steps away from the outdoor market, the Mercato Centrale awaits—a sprawling indoor food market that will make any food lover's heart race. Located on the second floor of the market building, this gastronomic wonderland is where Florence's culinary delights come to life. The scent of freshly baked focaccia, sizzling meats, and rich cheeses fill the air, enticing you to explore every corner. Here, you can sample traditional Tuscan fare, from juicy, flame-grilled bistecca alla Fiorentina (Florentine steak) to delicate truffle-infused pasta. Don't miss the chance to try a freshly made panino stuffed with prosciutto and pecorino, or indulge in a refreshing gelato. With each bite, you're savoring the authenticity of Tuscany—an unforgettable culinary experience that will leave you yearning for more.

Florentine Leather Goods: A visit to San Lorenzo Market wouldn't be complete without exploring its famed leather section. Florence has a centuries-old tradition of leather craftsmanship, and the market offers a stunning display of this artistry. As you stroll through the market, you'll be captivated by the array of leather goods on offer—from sleek handbags and stylish belts to jackets and wallets, all made with the finest Italian leather. What makes shopping for leather in San Lorenzo so special is the opportunity to meet the artisans themselves. Many of the leather goods vendors proudly showcase their craft, sharing the story behind each piece. The rich scent of leather fills the air as you run your fingers over the smooth, supple surfaces, and you're instantly drawn into the artistry and skill that make Florentine leather renowned worldwide.

The Vibrant Atmosphere of Local Life: San Lorenzo Market is more than just a tourist destination—it's a living, breathing part of Florentine life. As you wander through its maze of stalls and shops, you'll see locals mingling with tourists, bargaining for the best deals, and chatting with the vendors like old friends. This is a place where cultures meet, and the interactions are warm and genuine. Take a moment to sit at one of the nearby cafés and watch the world go by. You'll find yourself captivated by the rhythm of the market: the chatter of Italian voices, the clink of coins, the shuffle of feet across the cobblestones. It's the perfect place to experience the true spirit of Florence, where every corner offers a new discovery, and every encounter feels like a celebration of life.

4.7 Oltrarno Neighborhood

The Oltrarno neighborhood is Florence's hidden gem—a vibrant area where tradition meets innovation, and the past converges with the present. While the historic center of Florence draws the crowds, Oltrarno remains a tranquil, authentic slice of Florentine life, brimming with artisan workshops, lush gardens, and historical treasures. Here are captivating places in the Oltrarno that will stir your curiosity and invite you to uncover the soul of this charming district.

Pitti Palace: The majestic Pitti Palace, a former residence of the powerful Medici family, is one of the crown jewels of Oltrarno. As you walk through its imposing façade, you'll find yourself transported back to a time of opulence and grandeur. Inside, the palatial rooms, filled with lavish furnishings, ornate decorations, and priceless art collections, offer a fascinating glimpse into the lives of Florence's aristocracy. The Royal Apartments exude an air of elegance, while the Palatine Gallery showcases masterpieces by Raphael, Titian, and Rubens. Outside, the Boboli Gardens stretch over 45,000 square meters, offering a peaceful retreat with sculptures, fountains, and panoramic views of the city. Exploring the Pitti Palace is like stepping into a living museum of Renaissance art, architecture, and royal history.

Basilica di Santo Spirito: Tucked away in a quiet square, the Basilica di Santo Spirito is one of Florence's most serene and spiritually evocative churches. Designed by the great architect Filippo Brunelleschi, this humble yet beautiful basilica radiates calm, providing a stark contrast to the bustling streets of the city. The interior is filled with serene beauty, from the magnificent wooden crucifix by Michelangelo to the simple, yet captivating, altarpieces that adorn the chapels. The church also houses works by artists like Sandro Botticelli and Filippino Lippi, making it a lesser-known treasure trove of Renaissance art. The peaceful atmosphere of Santo Spirito invites quiet reflection and contemplation, offering a moment of tranquility in the midst of the vibrant Oltrarno.

Piazza del Carmine and the Brancacci Chapel: In the heart of Oltrarno lies the charming Piazza del Carmine, home to one of Florence's most revered artistic treasures—the Brancacci Chapel inside the Church of Santa Maria del Carmine. This small, unassuming chapel holds some of the most important frescoes of the early Renaissance, painted by Masaccio and Masolino. The Brancacci Chapel is often referred to as the "Sistine Chapel of the early Renaissance" due to the breathtaking beauty and groundbreaking techniques used in its frescoes. The most famous fresco, The Tribute Money, is a masterclass in perspective and human emotion. Stepping into this chapel is like stepping into a pivotal moment in the history of art, where the evolution of painting took a revolutionary turn.

Via Romana and the Artisan Workshops: One of the most charming aspects of the Oltrarno district is its vibrant artisan community, and there's no better place to experience this tradition than along Via Romana. As you stroll down this picturesque street, you'll encounter small workshops and studios where artisans continue centuries-old crafts, from hand-painted ceramics and leather goods to custom jewelry and restored antiques. The craftsmanship on display here is a testament to the skill and passion that Florentine artisans pour into their work. Stopping by these studios not only gives you a chance to purchase unique souvenirs, but it also offers a rare glimpse into the heart of Florence's artisanal heritage—something that's fast disappearing in the modern world.

Boboli Gardens: For a peaceful escape from the hustle and bustle of Florence, head to the Boboli Gardens, a sprawling green oasis behind the Pitti Palace. These grand gardens are a beautiful example of Italian Renaissance landscaping, offering a delightful mix of formal and naturalistic designs. As you wander through the shaded pathways, you'll encounter fountains, statues, and charming grottoes that make every corner of the garden feel like a scene from an old-world painting. The gardens offer some of the best panoramic views of Florence, with the city's terracotta rooftops stretching out beneath the Tuscan sky. Whether you're seeking a quiet place to relax or an opportunity to explore Florence from a different perspective, the Boboli Gardens provide a refreshing and peaceful retreat.

4.8 Piazzale Michelangelo

Piazzale Michelangelo is not just a square; it's a viewpoint, a celebration of art, and a place that beckons travelers to pause, reflect, and immerse themselves in the timeless beauty of Florence. Perched high on a hill, this remarkable spot offers sweeping panoramas of the city, making it a must-see destination for anyone visiting Florence. Here are unmissable experiences within Piazzale Michelangelo that will surely spark your curiosity and leave a lasting impression.

The Panoramic View of Florence: The first thing you'll notice as you step into Piazzale Michelangelo is the breathtaking panoramic view of Florence laid out before you. From this vantage point, the city looks almost like a painting, with the iconic red-tiled roofs, the majestic Duomo rising in the distance, and the graceful curves of the Arno River weaving through the landscape. As you stand there, the beauty of the city will captivate you, especially at sunset when the golden hues of the setting sun bathe Florence in a warm glow. Whether you're capturing the scene in a photograph or simply savoring the moment in silence, the view from Piazzale Michelangelo is an experience that transcends words. It's a chance to witness the stunning marriage of nature and architecture, making it one of the most unforgettable moments of your visit.

The Replica of Michelangelo's David: At the heart of Piazzale Michelangelo stands a replica of Michelangelo's David, one of the most celebrated sculptures in the world. The sheer presence of this masterpiece, even in replica form, is enough to leave you in awe. As you approach it, you'll notice the precision in the sculptor's attention to anatomical detail—the strength and grace of the figure seem almost alive. There's something deeply moving about witnessing David in this outdoor setting, with the panoramic city of Florence as his backdrop. It's a testament to the genius of Michelangelo and an opportunity to reflect on the power of art to immortalize the human spirit. As you stand in front of this iconic statue, you can't help but feel a sense of reverence for the artist's skill and the enduring beauty of his work.

The Gardens of the Boboli: A short walk from Piazzale Michelangelo leads you to the majestic Boboli Gardens, one of the most beautiful green spaces in Florence. These gardens, which stretch behind the Pitti Palace, are a haven of tranquility, with neatly manicured lawns, fountains, and sculptures scattered throughout. As you wander through the gardens, you'll discover hidden paths that lead to stunning viewpoints overlooking the city, as well as intricate sculptures that pay homage to Renaissance ideals. The gardens are a perfect place to escape the hustle and bustle of Florence, offering peace and quiet amid a backdrop of greenery and history. It's not just a garden; it's a living museum, where nature and art come together in perfect harmony.

The Church of San Miniato al Monte: A short walk uphill from Piazzale Michelangelo brings you to the Church of San Miniato al Monte, one of the most beautiful and serene churches in Florence. Perched on a hill, this Romanesque church offers an intimate and spiritual atmosphere, far removed from the crowds below. The church itself is a marvel of architecture, with its stunning facade and intricate interior, featuring mosaic work and frescoes that reflect the religious devotion of the time. As you step inside, you're immediately enveloped in a sense of calm, with the hushed reverence of the space inviting you to take a moment for reflection. The church also offers sweeping views of the city, providing a different perspective on Florence, one that blends history, religion, and art in a truly peaceful setting.

The Equestrian Statue of Cosimo I: Near the entrance of Piazzale Michelangelo stands the imposing equestrian statue of Cosimo I de' Medici, a symbol of the power and influence of the Medici family in Florence. Created by sculptor Giambologna in the late 16th century, this statue captures the grandeur and authority of Cosimo I, who was a central figure in the city's history. As you stand before the statue, you'll feel the weight of history, as if Cosimo I himself is still watching over the city he helped shape. The statue's grandeur and the surrounding views create an atmosphere of awe and reverence, offering a chance to reflect on Florence's rich political and cultural heritage. It's a powerful reminder of the city's past and a perfect spot to appreciate the historical significance of the Medici family's influence on Florence.

4.9 Santa Croce Basilica

Santa Croce Basilica is a place that resonates with history, art, and a profound sense of reverence. As you step inside, you are not merely visiting a church; you are entering a living testament to the city's rich past and spiritual legacy. Known for being the final resting place of some of Italy's greatest minds, Santa Croce offers much more than just its religious significance. Here are compelling places within and around the Basilica that will leave you in awe and inspire a deep connection with Florence's soul.

The Tomb of Michelangelo: The very name Michelangelo evokes visions of artistic masterpieces and revolutionary genius. Within the grand interior of Santa Croce, you'll find his tomb, a breathtaking monument dedicated to one of the most influential artists in history. The tomb, designed by the renowned sculptor Vincenzo Pacetti, is an imposing structure that speaks volumes about the man it honors. The monument is adorned with allegorical figures representing Painting, Sculpture, and Architecture, symbolizing Michelangelo's vast contributions to each of these fields. As you stand before his tomb, there is a palpable sense of awe and reverence. It's a quiet moment of reflection that underscores the timeless impact Michelangelo had on Florence—and the world.

The Pazzi Chapel: The Pazzi Chapel, located in the cloister of Santa Croce, is one of the finest examples of Renaissance architecture. Designed by Filippo Brunelleschi, the chapel exudes an understated elegance that highlights the genius of its creator. Its serene, symmetrical design, with its delicate arches and harmonious proportions, offers a visual reprieve from the bustling energy of the city. But what truly sets the Pazzi Chapel apart is its sense of tranquility. Standing in the space, surrounded by its perfect geometrical shapes, you can almost feel the weight of history resting on your shoulders. It's as if Brunelleschi's vision is still alive in the very walls of this architectural gem, making it a must-see for those who appreciate the depth of Florence's artistic legacy.

The Giotto's Frescoes: Giotto di Bondone's stunning frescoes inside the Chapel of the Peruzzi are one of the most moving sights in Santa Croce. These works, dating back to the early 14th century, depict the life of St. John the Baptist and St. John the Evangelist with a realism and emotional depth that were revolutionary for their time. Giotto's ability to convey raw human emotion through his figures set the stage for the development of Renaissance art, and as you gaze upon these frescoes, you are transported to a world where divinity and humanity intertwine. The vivid scenes capture moments of spiritual significance, yet they are infused with a sense of intimacy and tenderness that make them feel timeless and universal.

The Tomb of Galileo Galilei: If Michelangelo's tomb represents the artistic spirit of Florence, then the tomb of Galileo Galilei, located near the main altar, stands as a tribute to the intellectual and scientific achievements that shaped the modern world. Galileo, the father of modern science, made revolutionary discoveries that changed our understanding of the universe. His tomb within Santa Croce is a powerful reminder of Florence's role as a cradle of scientific thought. The monument itself is simple but dignified, and standing before it, you can't help but feel the weight of Galileo's legacy. The knowledge that such a pioneering figure is honored here only deepens your appreciation of the Basilica as a place of both spiritual and intellectual importance.

The Cloisters of Santa Croce: The Cloisters of Santa Croce offer a peaceful, meditative escape from the crowds outside. These serene courtyards, with their gently arched columns and beautifully landscaped gardens, provide a quiet sanctuary where visitors can reflect and absorb the historical significance of the church. The cloisters are often overlooked by the casual tourist, but they are a hidden treasure that offers an intimate connection with the church's monastic past. As you walk along the stone paths, beneath the shade of ancient trees, it's easy to imagine the monks who once wandered here in contemplation. The tranquility of the cloisters creates a gentle atmosphere, encouraging a sense of inner peace that contrasts beautifully with the busy energy of Florence.

4.10 Florence Baptistery

One of the most unforgettable sights in the Florence Baptistery is the iconic Gates of Paradise, designed by Lorenzo Ghiberti. These magnificent bronze doors, with their intricate biblical scenes, are truly a marvel to behold. The name "Gates of Paradise" was coined by Michelangelo, who, upon seeing them, described them as so beautiful that they appeared as though they were gates to heaven itself. As you stand before them, you can trace the delicate details of each panel, each depicting a scene from the Old Testament with a stunning blend of realism and symbolism. The golden sheen of the bronze catches the light in a way that seems to breathe life into these biblical stories, drawing you into a moment suspended in time. The grandeur of these doors serves as a powerful reminder of Florence's artistic legacy, inviting you to explore the rich connection between art, religion, and human creativity.

The Intricacies of the Baptistery Ceiling: As you step into the Baptistery, look up, and you'll be immediately captivated by the stunning mosaic that covers the entire ceiling. This radiant work, dating back to the 13th century, depicts the Last Judgment, a powerful and awe-inspiring scene of heaven and hell. The golden background creates a heavenly glow, while the rich details of angels, saints, and sinners pull you into a spiritual journey. The scale and intricacy of the mosaic are overwhelming, as each figure seems to come alive, offering a glimpse into the medieval worldview of divine judgment. Standing beneath this celestial masterpiece, you can almost feel the weight of eternity pressing down, reminding you of the timeless nature of faith, sin, and salvation. It's a moving experience, both visually and emotionally, urging you to contemplate the spiritual history that has shaped Florence.

The Baptismal Font: At the heart of the Florence Baptistery lies the baptismal font, where countless Florentines have been baptized over the centuries. This simple yet sacred space invites reflection on the rituals and traditions that have been passed down through generations. The font, made of marble and adorned with reliefs depicting scenes from the life of St. John the Baptist, is a symbol of rebirth and spiritual purification. The solemnity of this space, coupled with its rich history, provides visitors with an intimate glimpse into the religious practices that have shaped the city for centuries. Whether you're a pilgrim or a casual visitor, standing near the font evokes a sense of connection to the generations who have walked through these hallowed doors before you, making it a deeply personal experience.

The Baptistery's Architectural Grandeur: The Baptistery itself is an architectural gem, showcasing the grandeur of Romanesque design. Its octagonal shape and vast marble columns create a sense of openness and tranquility, while the elegant proportions of the structure invite admiration. As you explore the interior, take note of the beautiful inlaid marble floors, with their intricate geometric patterns that guide you through the sacred space. The

Baptistery's design reflects a harmonious blend of spirituality and architectural ingenuity, with each detail carefully considered to create a space that feels both sacred and awe-inspiring. Walking through its doors, you can't help but feel transported back to a time when this space was at the heart of Florence's religious and civic life. The Baptistery is not just a building; it's a testament to the ingenuity and devotion of those who constructed it, and standing in its presence is a humbling experience.

CHAPTER 5
HIDDEN GEMS AND LOCAL FAVORITES

5.1 Off-the-Beaten-Path Neighborhoods

Florence often lures travelers to its famous landmarks like the Duomo, Uffizi Gallery, and Ponte Vecchio. However, for those seeking a more intimate and authentic side of the city, stepping away from the crowded tourist hotspots reveals hidden treasures that tell a different story of Florence. These lesser-known neighborhoods offer an escape into the city's soul, where quiet streets, local flavors, and unique landmarks wait to be discovered. Here are off-the-beaten-path neighborhoods in Florence, each with its own charm and character, promising a deeply enriching experience for any traveler.

San Niccolò: Just below the towering fortress of Forte di Belvedere, the San Niccolò district offers a peaceful retreat from the usual hustle and bustle of Florence. This area is often overlooked by tourists, but those who venture here are rewarded with cobbled streets, authentic trattorias, and a magnificent view of the city that few get to see. The highlight of San Niccolò is the climb up to Piazzale Michelangelo, where the panoramic vistas over the Arno River, Florence's terracotta rooftops, and the Tuscan hills beyond will take your breath away. Take a stroll along the ancient walls, stopping at quaint shops selling local crafts, and you'll feel like you're stepping into a storybook.

Sant'Ambrogio: For a taste of the true Florentine lifestyle, the Sant'Ambrogio district offers a delightful immersion into local life. Here, the central market, Mercato di Sant'Ambrogio, is a bustling hub where locals shop for fresh produce, cheeses, meats, and traditional delicacies. While the market is a popular spot for foodies, it feels worlds apart from the more touristy Mercato Centrale. The neighborhood itself is brimming with charm, with narrow streets leading to hidden courtyards and charming cafes serving up authentic Tuscan dishes. It's a perfect place to sit back with a glass of Chianti, savoring simple, delicious food while observing the daily rhythm of Florentine life.

Campo di Marte: Not far from the center, Campo di Marte is a neighborhood that offers a completely different side of Florence. Known for its sports culture, it's where you'll find the Artemio Franchi Stadium, home to the Florence football club, ACF Fiorentina. While the stadium itself is a magnet for sports fans, the surrounding area is a lovely blend of residential streets and peaceful green spaces. This quieter part of the city is perfect for those seeking a break from the crowds. Enjoy a leisurely walk through the Giardino dell'Orticoltura, a beautiful public garden with well-maintained flower beds, palm trees, and a charming greenhouse. With fewer tourists around, Campo di Marte gives you an opportunity to see Florence through the eyes of a local.

Le Cure: If you've ever wondered where the locals live, Le Cure offers a glimpse into the daily lives of Florentines away from the tourist trail. Located just northeast of the city center, this residential neighborhood is a patchwork of historic buildings, quiet streets, and small parks. One of the gems of this area is the Giardino di Villa Strozzi, a hidden garden that's often overlooked by visitors. This peaceful space is perfect for a relaxing afternoon, offering shaded paths, lush greenery, and occasional cultural events. Le Cure also has a vibrant local market where you can sample fresh Tuscan produce, and if you're lucky, catch a glimpse of traditional street festivals. The area retains a down-to-earth, community-focused feel, making it an ideal destination for travelers seeking to experience the real Florence.

5.2 Local Markets and Shopping Streets

Florence is a city that weaves the past and present into a rich tapestry of culture, there's something equally captivating about wandering through Florence's bustling local markets and charming shopping streets. These places offer not only a peek into the everyday life of the Florentines but also the chance to find unique treasures that you won't find anywhere else. If you're planning a trip, make sure to carve out time to explore these vibrant spots. Here are places that should be on your must-see list.

Mercato Centrale: Located in the heart of San Lorenzo, the Mercato Centrale is a paradise for food lovers. The market is housed in a magnificent 19th-century building, where you'll find two levels brimming with local delicacies. The ground floor is dedicated to the traditional market experience, with vendors selling fresh produce, meats, cheeses, and vibrant flowers. The air is thick with the scent of cured meats, ripe fruits, and freshly baked bread. The upper floor of the Mercato Centrale is a modern food court, offering a more contemporary take on Italian cuisine. Here, you can savor everything from gourmet pizzas and handmade pastas to Tuscan specialties like lampredotto (a local sandwich made from cow's stomach). The market is more than just a place to buy food—it's an immersive experience where you can sit down and taste the very essence of Florence. As you wander between the stalls, don't forget to stop and chat with the passionate vendors—they're always eager to share stories and recipes from their heritage.

Via de' Tornabuoni: For those with an eye for fashion, Via de' Tornabuoni is Florence's premier shopping street, lined with high-end boutiques and designer stores. This elegant street, named after one of the city's most illustrious noble families, has become a symbol of Florence's status as a hub of style and luxury. Here, you can shop for the latest collections from renowned Italian designers like Gucci, Salvatore Ferragamo, and Prada, all of which call Florence their home. While the prices may be steep, simply strolling along Via de' Tornabuoni is an experience in itself. The opulent storefronts and the chic atmosphere of this district make you feel as though you've stepped into a world of timeless Italian fashion. The surrounding architecture, with its Renaissance buildings and grand palaces, only adds to the feeling of walking through a fashion-forward open-air museum.

Mercato di San Lorenzo: Just a short walk from the Mercato Centrale, the Mercato di San Lorenzo is another iconic spot that captures the essence of

Florence. This market, especially known for its leather goods, is the perfect place to find authentic Tuscan souvenirs. From handcrafted leather jackets and bags to belts and wallets, you'll be tempted by the smell of freshly tanned leather wafting through the air. Beyond leather, the market also offers an array of local artisan products, such as hand-painted ceramics, delicate lacework, and Tuscan olive oil. It's a wonderful spot to find unique keepsakes that carry the spirit of the city. The market's vibrant stalls are often buzzing with friendly haggling, and there's always something new to discover—whether it's a beautifully crafted piece of jewelry or a handwoven scarf. The lively atmosphere and the warm smiles of the vendors make it a place you'll want to return to time and again.

Piazza del Mercato Nuovo: Piazza del Mercato Nuovo, located near the Ponte Vecchio, is a picturesque square that was once the site of Florence's historic wool market. Today, it's a great place to shop for souvenirs with a unique Florentine twist. The most iconic item you'll encounter here is the "porcellino," a bronze wild boar statue. It's believed that rubbing its nose will bring good luck, so don't forget to do so before making your way through the market. The shops surrounding the square are filled with vendors offering a range of Florentine goods, from leather handbags to jewelry, and even colorful scarves. The atmosphere here is relaxed yet bustling, making it the perfect spot to pick up gifts or simply enjoy the charm of the market. The area is also great for a quick break in one of the nearby cafés, where you can sit back and soak in the lively ambiance.

5.3 Authentic Trattorias and Restaurants

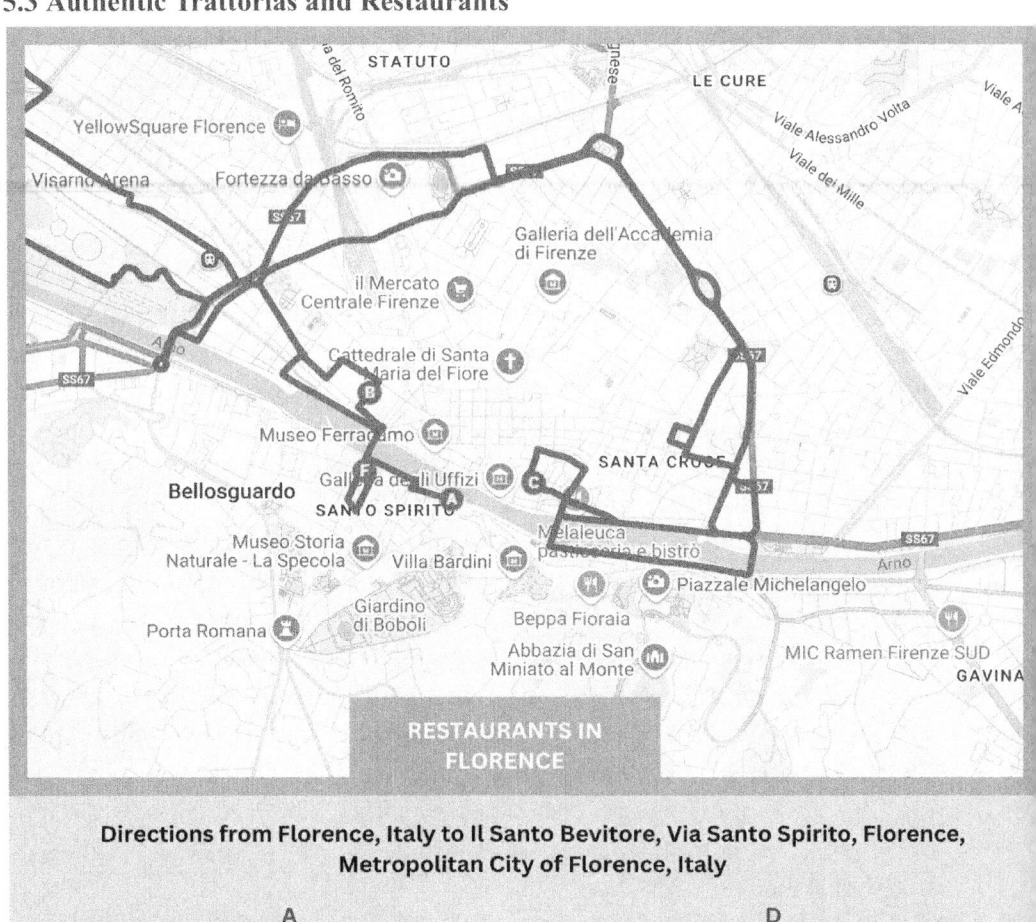

RESTAURANTS IN FLORENCE

Directions from Florence, Italy to Il Santo Bevitore, Via Santo Spirito, Florence, Metropolitan City of Florence, Italy

A
Florence, Italy

B
Trattoria Sostanza, Via del Porcellana, Florence, Metropolitan City of Florence, Italy

C
All'Antico Vinaio, Via dei Neri, Florence, Metropolitan City of Florence, Italy

D
Cibrèo Trattoria, Via dei Macci, Florence, Metropolitan City of Florence, Italy

E
Ristorante Trattoria da Burde, Via Pistoiese, Florence, Metropolitan City of Florence, Italy

F
Il Santo Bevitore, Via Santo Spirito, Florence, Metropolitan City of Florence, Italy

Dining here is an immersive experience that connects you to the heart of Tuscan traditions. The trattorias and restaurants in Florence are more than places to eat—they are sanctuaries of flavor, steeped in history and the pride of local chefs who craft their dishes with the utmost passion and care. Below, I'll take you on a journey through authentic dining spots that promise to not only satisfy your hunger but ignite a deeper curiosity about the tastes of this magical city.

Trattoria Sostanza: Tucked away near the bustling Via della Porcellana, Trattoria Sostanza is an institution in Florence, and for good reason. Founded in 1869, this place carries the weight of tradition while offering an intimate and rustic dining experience. The moment you step inside, you are greeted by an atmosphere that radiates history—wooden beams, antique furniture, and a warmth that makes you feel like part of the family. The food here is unpretentious but bursting with flavor, with the pollo al burro (butter chicken) being their crowning jewel. This dish, cooked to perfection, will make your taste buds sing and remind you of the simple beauty of Tuscan cooking. Dining at Sostanza is like walking through the doors of time, where the past meets the present on your plate.

Osteria All'Antico Vinaio: No list of authentic eateries would be complete without Osteria All'Antico Vinaio, an iconic spot in Florence that's renowned for its sandwiches. This humble osteria might not look like much from the outside, but its schiacciata (Tuscan flatbread) filled with cured meats, cheeses, and seasonal vegetables is nothing short of a revelation. With a glass of Tuscan wine in hand, you'll savor the art of simple yet divine flavors. The energy here is infectious—locals and tourists alike gather in this quaint corner of Florence to indulge in the legendary sandwiches that have earned this place fame worldwide. The unassuming exterior hides a culinary masterpiece, and that's what makes it so special.

Cibrèo: Cibrèo offers an elegant but still deeply traditional approach to Tuscan cuisine. Located in the heart of Florence, this restaurant has gained an almost mythical reputation, and it's easy to see why. The menu here is a celebration of the authentic flavors of Tuscany, yet Chef Fabio Picchi brings a modern twist that feels both inventive and respectful to the region's culinary roots. Don't miss their signature ribollita, a hearty Tuscan vegetable soup, or the exquisite torta della nonna for dessert, which showcases the delicate sweetness of Tuscan pastries. Dining at Cibrèo feels like an exploration of Tuscany's past, present, and future in every bite—a perfect fusion of rustic charm and refined dining.

Trattoria da Burde: For those who seek a genuine Florentine dining experience, Trattoria da Burde is a true gem. This trattoria is famous for its hearty, soulful dishes that have been perfected over generations. Located a little outside the city center, this family-run spot is beloved by Florentines for its authenticity. Here, you can enjoy a plate of bistecca alla fiorentina (Florentine steak), grilled to perfection and served with a side of roasted potatoes. The atmosphere is warm and welcoming, with generations of Florentine families enjoying their meals alongside curious travelers. The flavors are bold, rich, and comforting, and each dish carries a sense of family tradition that makes the experience unforgettable.

Il Santo Bevitore: Il Santo Bevitore offers an inviting and stylish atmosphere with a commitment to both tradition and innovation. Nestled in a charming street just south of the Arno River, this restaurant showcases the creativity of modern Italian cooking while paying homage to Tuscany's culinary roots. Their pappardelle with wild boar ragu is a standout, combining the earthiness of the boar with the delicate texture of the homemade pasta. The restaurant is ideal for those who want to experience something more contemporary yet deeply rooted in Florence's food heritage. Whether you're enjoying a glass of wine from their extensive selection or savoring a plate of tiramisu, the flavors here will leave a lasting impression.

5.4 Wine Bars and Enoteche
Florence offers a treasure trove of experiences. For wine enthusiasts, this enchanting city holds a particular allure, with its delightful wine bars and enoteche (wine cellars) that celebrate the finest Tuscan wines. Here are must-visit places in Florence that not only promise exceptional wines but offer an intimate experience that lingers in your heart long after you've taken your last sip.

Le Volpi e l'Uva: Tucked away on a charming street near the Ponte Vecchio, Le Volpi e l'Uva stands as a beacon of Tuscan wine excellence. With its unassuming exterior, you might miss it if you weren't looking closely—but that's what makes this place so special. Inside, it's a cozy haven filled with an extensive selection of regional wines. The intimate atmosphere allows you to have a personal conversation with the staff, who are not only knowledgeable but also passionate about sharing their love for local wines. You can sample a glass of Chianti Classico, perhaps accompanied by local cheeses and salami, and feel transported to the rolling hills of Tuscany. A visit here is a journey into the heart of Italy's winemaking tradition, and it's impossible not to feel the warmth of the Tuscan spirit with each sip.

Enoteca Pitti Gola e Cantina: Located just below the grand Pitti Palace, Enoteca Pitti Gola e Cantina is where art meets wine. The wine list here reads like a love letter to the region, featuring some of the finest Tuscan wines. Step inside, and you're enveloped in an ambiance that perfectly reflects Florence's Renaissance roots: elegant, yet approachable. The knowledgeable staff is ready to guide you through a tasting experience that blends wine with history. Pair your glass of Brunello di Montalcino with Tuscan delicacies such as truffle-based dishes or a simple plate of pappardelle with wild boar sauce. Every visit to this enoteca feels like stepping into an artist's studio where each bottle of wine is treated as a masterpiece. It's the perfect place to savor the essence of Florence, one glass at a time.

Il Santo Bevitore: If you're looking for a place where contemporary flair meets Tuscan tradition, Il Santo Bevitore is the place to be. Situated in the San Frediano district, this wine bar is celebrated not only for its remarkable collection of wines but also for its modern yet warm atmosphere. The rustic charm, combined with sleek design elements, creates an inviting environment to relax and indulge in a glass of wine. The menu is a fusion of Tuscan tradition and creative innovation, featuring dishes like roasted lamb with rosemary and decadent chocolate tarts. But what truly steals the show is the wine list—featuring both well-known labels and hidden gems. The staff's passion for wine shines through as they encourage you to try wines from lesser-known regions of Tuscany, providing you with a tasting experience that's both educational and utterly delightful.

Caffè degli Artigiani: For a wine bar that also serves as an artistic retreat, Caffè degli Artigiani offers a unique experience. Nestled in the Oltrarno neighborhood, this charming enoteca has a laid-back vibe, making it perfect for those seeking a more casual yet equally engaging wine experience. The wine list here is thoughtfully curated, with a particular focus on organic wines from small, family-owned vineyards. The warm, rustic interior with its mix of wooden tables and contemporary art on the walls adds an eclectic touch, making it a great place to unwind after a day of sightseeing. Don't miss the opportunity to try their signature cocktail made with Tuscan vin santo—it's a perfect representation of the region's creativity and flair for blending tradition with innovation.

Enoteca Cantinetta Antinori: A name synonymous with Tuscan excellence, the Antinori family has been at the forefront of winemaking for centuries, and their enoteca in Florence offers a chance to taste their legendary wines in a setting that matches their status. Located near the famous Piazza della Signoria, this wine bar is a true tribute to Tuscany's vinous heritage. As you step inside, you are welcomed by a sleek, contemporary interior that contrasts with the centuries-old family tradition behind it. The wine list features a selection of Antinori wines that showcase the family's storied history in winemaking, from their bold, complex Super Tuscans to their refined Chianti Classico. Pair these exceptional wines with dishes like truffle risotto or a plate of pecorino cheese, and you'll understand why this enoteca is a must-visit for wine connoisseurs. The combination of exceptional wine and elegant surroundings makes for an unforgettable experience.

5.5 Secret Gardens and Parks
These secret oases in the heart of Florence are perfect for those seeking tranquility, natural beauty, and an authentic Florentine experience. Here are enchanting gardens and parks in Florence that will stir your curiosity and leave you longing to explore more.

Boboli Gardens: The Boboli Gardens, located behind the Pitti Palace, are among the most famous in Florence, yet they still manage to preserve an air of hidden wonder. Designed in the 16th century for the powerful Medici family, these expansive gardens are a perfect blend of nature, art, and history. As you wander through the meticulously manicured pathways, the scent of blooming flowers and the sight of sculptures, fountains, and grottos invite you to step into a world of timeless beauty. One of the most captivating aspects of the Boboli Gardens is the stunning view it offers of Florence. From the top of the garden's hills, you can gaze over the terracotta rooftops and the iconic Duomo, framed by the surrounding hills of Tuscany. The garden feels like a living piece of art, with each corner revealing something new, whether it's a quiet, hidden fountain or a secluded terrace draped in ivy. For anyone who appreciates both nature and history, the Boboli Gardens are an unmissable part of Florence's green heart.

Rose Garden (Giardino delle Rose): Just a short walk from the famous Piazzale Michelangelo, lies the charming Giardino delle Rose (Rose Garden). Overlooking the Arno River and the city's iconic skyline, this lesser-known garden offers a peaceful escape with stunning views. In the spring and summer, the garden bursts into color as hundreds of rose varieties bloom, filling the air with sweet fragrance. The garden is also home to other flowers, sculptures, and even a collection of bonsai trees. What makes the Rose Garden so special is its intimate and tranquil atmosphere. It's a perfect spot to unwind, take a leisurely stroll, or sit on one of the benches and watch the sunset over the city. The combination of its serene beauty, the panoramic views, and the soothing sounds of nature makes this park an ideal location for a quiet afternoon, away from the crowds. The Rose Garden feels like a well-kept secret, a sanctuary in the midst of Florence's lively streets.

Iris Garden (Giardino dell'Iris): Another hidden gem in Florence is the Iris Garden, located near the historical San Miniato al Monte. Open only in the spring, this garden is dedicated to the cultivation of the iris flower, and its 2,000 varieties make it one of the most significant iris gardens in the world. The garden's vibrant colors and intoxicating fragrance create a sensory experience like no other. What sets the Iris Garden apart is its serenity and seclusion. Tucked away in the hills, with views of the city and the Tuscan countryside, the garden provides a peaceful and romantic setting.

CHAPTER 6
DAY TRIPS AND EXCURSIONS

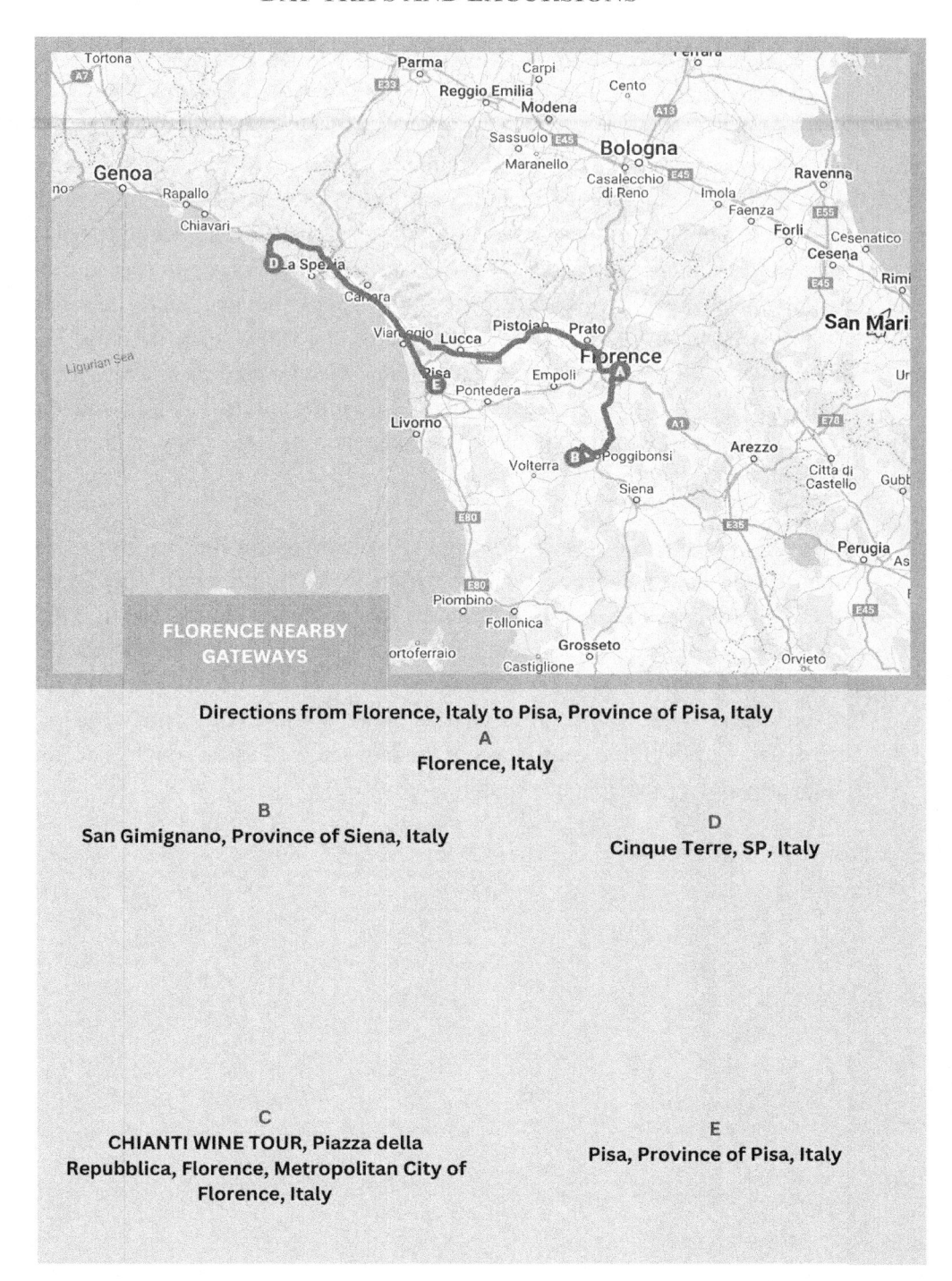

FLORENCE NEARBY GATEWAYS

Directions from Florence, Italy to Pisa, Province of Pisa, Italy

A
Florence, Italy

B
San Gimignano, Province of Siena, Italy

D
Cinque Terre, SP, Italy

C
CHIANTI WINE TOUR, Piazza della Repubblica, Florence, Metropolitan City of Florence, Italy

E
Pisa, Province of Pisa, Italy

79

6.1 Siena and San Gimignano

Florence offers a wide range of day trips that transport visitors into the region's timeless charm. Among the most popular excursions are those that lead to Siena and San Gimignano, two of Tuscany's most beloved towns. These day trips provide a stunning glimpse into the region's history, art, architecture, and natural beauty, offering a perfect escape from the bustling streets of Florence. Here, we will explore these excursions, providing details about the distance, cost of transportation, what to expect, and other essential information to ensure an unforgettable experience.

The Allure of Siena: A trip from Florence to Siena is a journey that immerses travelers in the medieval spirit of Tuscany. Situated about 75 kilometers (47 miles) south of Florence, Siena is a UNESCO World Heritage site renowned for its well-preserved medieval architecture and vibrant history. The trip to Siena by car takes roughly an hour and a half, making it an ideal destination for a full-day excursion. For those opting for public transportation, buses and trains are readily available. The bus ride from Florence to Siena takes approximately 1.5 hours, with one-way tickets typically costing around 8 to 12 euros. Alternatively, a train ride from Florence's Santa Maria Novella station to Siena requires a transfer at Empoli, with a total travel time of about 1.5 to 2 hours, and tickets costing approximately 12 to 15 euros. Visitors can also choose a guided tour, which often includes transportation, with prices ranging from 40 to 80 euros per person depending on the inclusivity of the tour. Upon arrival in Siena, visitors are greeted by the sight of Piazza del Campo, one of the most beautiful medieval squares in the world. The square, home to the famous Palio horse race, is surrounded by charming cafes and historic buildings. A visit to the Palazzo Pubblico, the town hall, and the Torre del Mangia, a towering medieval bell tower, provides a perfect opportunity to marvel at Siena's artistic and architectural splendor. From here, visitors can wander the narrow, winding streets, where every corner reveals a glimpse of the town's rich history.

Exploring San Gimignano: From Siena, a short 30-minute drive or bus ride will bring travelers to San Gimignano, a picturesque hilltop town that looks like something straight out of a medieval fairy tale. San Gimignano, located about 50 kilometers (31 miles) from Siena, is famous for its medieval towers that pierce the sky, earning it the nickname "The Town of Fine Towers." The town is a striking example of medieval urbanism, and its skyline, composed of 13 surviving towers (once there were 72), remains an awe-inspiring sight. San Gimignano is easily accessible from Florence by car, with a drive taking about an hour and a half. Public transportation options include buses, which depart regularly from Florence's central bus station and reach San Gimignano in approximately 1.5 hours. Bus tickets typically cost around 10 to 15 euros. Visitors can also opt for a guided tour that may combine Siena and San Gimignano, offering a more in-depth look at both towns, with prices generally ranging from 50 to 90 euros per person.

The Scenic Drive: The journey between Florence, Siena, and San Gimignano is a true pleasure for the senses. Traveling by car offers the freedom to explore the Tuscan countryside at a leisurely pace, with picturesque rolling hills, vineyards, and olive groves surrounding every turn. For those driving, the route between Florence and Siena is approximately 75 kilometers, and the drive to San Gimignano from Siena covers another 50 kilometers. Both routes offer scenic views of the Tuscan landscape, making the journey itself an essential part of the experience. Along the way, visitors can stop in charming Tuscan villages, sample local wines, and enjoy the region's famed cuisine. The road from Florence to Siena winds through the Chianti region, known for its world-class vineyards and olive oil production. Travelers can stop at local wineries for a tasting of the region's renowned Chianti Classico wines, accompanied by artisanal cheeses and meats.

Practical Information: When planning a day trip from Florence to Siena and San Gimignano, it's essential to consider timing and logistics. A full day is recommended to fully appreciate both towns, as they each have much to offer. Many visitors opt for organized day tours that include transportation, guided tours, and sometimes meals. These tours typically start early in the morning and return to Florence by evening, ensuring a full and enriching day. For those traveling independently, it's important to wear comfortable shoes, as both Siena and San Gimignano are built on hilly terrain, and walking is the best way to explore these historic towns. Also, during peak tourist seasons, especially in summer, these towns can get quite crowded, so it's advisable to arrive early to avoid the crowds and make the most of the experience. In terms of costs, a day trip to Siena and San Gimignano can vary depending on the mode of transportation. For public transportation, visitors can expect to pay around 15 to 30 euros for a round-trip bus or train ticket. Renting a car for the day may cost anywhere from 40 to 100 euros, depending on the car model and rental agency. Guided tours generally range from 50 to 90 euros per person, offering a hassle-free way to experience both towns in one day.

6.2 Pisa and Lucca

Florence serves as a perfect starting point for travelers eager to explore the stunning gems of Tuscany. Among the most sought-after day trips from Florence are the historic cities of Pisa and Lucca. While these two cities offer contrasting atmospheres, each of them offers its own unique charm and a wealth of experiences. The excursion from Florence to these picturesque towns takes visitors through the scenic Tuscan countryside, giving them a chance to immerse themselves in the region's rich heritage. Here, we will explore what to expect when embarking on day trips to Pisa and Lucca, including details on transportation, distances, and the unforgettable sights that await you.

The Journey to Pisa: A day trip from Florence to Pisa is an iconic Tuscan experience, and it begins with a relatively short but scenic journey. The distance between Florence and Pisa is approximately 85 kilometers, a mere 1.5-hour train ride. Trains leave frequently from Florence's Santa Maria Novella station and head straight to Pisa Centrale, with options ranging from quick regional trains to slower, more leisurely routes. The cost of the train ticket is modest, typically ranging between €8 to €15 for a one-way journey, depending on the type of train chosen and the class of service. As you arrive at Pisa, visitors are immediately drawn to the city's crown jewel: the Piazza dei Miracoli, or the Square of

Miracles. This UNESCO World Heritage site is home to some of the most extraordinary examples of medieval art and architecture, with the Leaning Tower of Pisa being the most famous. Expect to find a bustling square filled with tourists from around the world, all gathering to marvel at the Leaning Tower, which, despite its tilt, remains an engineering marvel. You can purchase tickets to climb the tower or simply enjoy its majestic beauty from the surrounding grassy lawns. Beyond the Leaning Tower, Pisa's cathedral, the Duomo di Pisa, and the Baptistery of St. John are also notable highlights. Visitors can take a moment to admire the intricate artwork and stunning architecture of these ancient structures. The city's atmosphere is one of a kind, where history and modern-day life blend seamlessly. When you've explored the major monuments, consider wandering through the charming streets of Pisa, lined with cozy cafes and shops offering local handicrafts. The local cuisine, including fresh pasta and Tuscan wines, is also a must-try during your time here.

A Journey to Lucca: While Pisa is often regarded for its world-renowned Leaning Tower, a day trip to Lucca offers a completely different experience. Located about 75 kilometers west of Florence, Lucca is a small but enchanting town that captivates visitors with its well-preserved medieval walls, cobblestone streets, and scenic views. The journey from Florence to Lucca by train takes just over an hour, and like the trip to Pisa, tickets cost around €8 to €15 one-way, with trains departing frequently throughout the day. Lucca is often overlooked in favor of its more famous Tuscan neighbors, but its tranquility and historical charm are precisely what make it such an appealing destination for those looking to escape the hustle and bustle of Florence. Upon arrival, visitors are immediately struck by the city's unique feature: the 4.2-kilometer-long Renaissance-era city walls. These towering walls, which once served as a form of defense, are now a delightful park that encircles the city. Visitors can take a leisurely stroll or rent a bike to ride around the walls, offering panoramic views of Lucca's charming rooftops and the surrounding Tuscan hills. Within the town, Lucca is dotted with remarkable medieval architecture, such as the striking Piazza dell'Anfiteatro, a round square built on the site of a Roman amphitheater. Walking through the narrow streets, you will find shops selling artisanal products, from leather goods to antiques, alongside quaint cafes where you can savor a coffee while watching the world go by. The town is also home to several beautiful churches, including the Basilica di San Frediano, which boasts a stunning golden mosaic on its façade, and the Cathedral of San Martino, renowned for its impressive marble façade and rich history.

Combining the Best of Pisa and Lucca: For those who wish to explore both Pisa and Lucca in a single day, it is entirely feasible, though the experience will be a whirlwind. The two cities are located relatively close to each other, with a driving distance of about 30 kilometers. The most convenient way to combine both destinations is to travel by train from Florence to Pisa in the morning, spend a few hours touring the Piazza dei Miracoli and surrounding areas, and then hop on a train to Lucca in the early afternoon. The train journey between Pisa and Lucca takes around 30 minutes, making it a quick and easy transition between the two. While in Lucca, visitors can enjoy a leisurely stroll along the city walls, take in the views from Guinigi Tower, and savor the local cuisine before returning to Florence in the evening. For those who prefer not to rush, it is also possible to split the trips across two days, allowing for a more relaxed exploration of both towns.

Transportation and Practical Tips: Traveling between Florence, Pisa, and Lucca is simple and efficient, thanks to Tuscany's excellent rail network. Tickets for regional trains can be purchased at the station or online through the Trenitalia website, with many options for discount fares if purchased in advance. The cost of train tickets is affordable, with the average round-trip fare between Florence and Pisa or Lucca ranging from €16 to €30, depending on the specific route and class of service. If you prefer to travel by car, the drive between the cities is straightforward, though finding parking in the historic centers can be challenging, so it is advisable to book parking in advance if traveling by car. When planning your day trip, it's important to be mindful of the opening hours for the major attractions in both Pisa and Lucca. Many of the monuments and museums in both cities close for a few hours during the afternoon, so it is recommended to arrive early in the day to make the most of your time.

6.3 Chianti Wine Region

The Chianti wine region is one of Italy's most celebrated destinations for wine lovers and nature enthusiasts alike. Just a short distance from the hustle and bustle of Florence, a visit to this picturesque landscape offers a serene escape into rolling hills, ancient vineyards, and charming medieval towns. For those seeking an authentic Tuscan experience, a day trip to Chianti is a must. This journey offers not only the chance to explore world-renowned wineries but also to experience the region's rich cultural heritage, stunning views, and delightful culinary traditions.

Getting to Chianti from Florence: The Chianti region is easily accessible from Florence, with several transportation options available. The distance from Florence to the heart of Chianti varies depending on the specific destination within the region, but on average, it takes around 45 minutes to 1.5 hours by car, covering approximately 30 to 50 kilometers. If you prefer a more leisurely approach, taking a guided tour is a popular choice. Many local tour operators offer day trips that include transportation in comfortable vehicles, often with air-conditioning, making the journey both convenient and pleasant. The cost for a guided tour typically ranges from 80 to 150 euros per person, depending on the inclusions such as wine tastings, meals, and extra activities. For those opting to drive themselves, car rentals in Florence are available for about 40 to 80 euros per day, though it's important to note that some parts of Chianti's winding roads can be narrow and winding, adding an adventurous touch to the trip.

Wine Tastings and Vineyard Tours: The allure of Chianti lies in its sprawling vineyards, which produce some of the most sought-after wines in the world. As you venture deeper into the region, expect to encounter a variety of picturesque wineries, each offering a unique insight into the winemaking process. Many wineries in Chianti provide guided tours of their cellars, where visitors can learn about the history of the region, the techniques used in crafting the wines, and the significance of the Sangiovese grape that dominates the local vineyards. The cost of a wine tasting experience typically ranges from 20 to 50 euros per person, with most tours lasting between 1 to 2 hours. What makes these visits particularly special is the opportunity to sample wines that are rarely found outside of Tuscany. During a wine tasting, you'll be introduced to the delicate nuances of Chianti Classico, the region's signature wine, as well as other local varieties like Vin Santo and Chianti Riserva. Some vineyards even offer the chance to pair wines with local delicacies, such as pecorino cheese, cured meats, and freshly baked bread. As you sip on your glass of Chianti, you'll be surrounded by the lush greenery of the hills, with the scent of ripening grapes filling the air. The panoramic views of the countryside, dotted with cypress trees and small stone villages, provide an unforgettable backdrop to this experience.

Exploring the Villages of Chianti: A visit to Chianti is not just about wine – it's about immersing yourself in the region's rich history and culture. The small medieval towns and villages that scatter the Chianti landscape offer a glimpse into Tuscany's past, with their cobbled streets, ancient churches, and historic landmarks. Towns like Greve in Chianti, Radda in Chianti, and Castellina in Chianti are popular stops on day trips from Florence, each offering its own charm. Greve in Chianti, often referred to as the gateway to Chianti, is home to a lovely square lined with local shops and eateries. Here, visitors can explore the historic Church of Santa Croce, which dates back to the 14th century, or take a leisurely walk around the town's vineyards. Radda in Chianti, perched on a hilltop, boasts panoramic views of the surrounding countryside and is known for its medieval fortress and quaint alleys. Castellina in Chianti is another gem, where visitors can wander through its charming streets and explore the ancient Etruscan tombs that are scattered around the area. The drive through these villages is as enchanting as the towns themselves, with winding roads that take you through olive groves and vineyards, each bend revealing yet another stunning view of the Tuscan hills. The cost of a visit to these villages is typically free, though some sites, like the Castellina Archaeological Museum or Greve's wine museum, may charge a small entry fee of 5 to 10 euros. Exploring the villages at a leisurely pace allows you to soak in the atmosphere and truly appreciate the beauty of this timeless region.

A Culinary Adventure: No trip to Chianti would be complete without indulging in its culinary offerings. The region is home to a rich gastronomic tradition that goes hand in hand with its winemaking heritage. Many of the vineyards and wineries offer the opportunity to enjoy a traditional Tuscan lunch or dinner, prepared with fresh, locally sourced ingredients. Expect to savor hearty dishes such as pappa al pomodoro (a thick tomato and bread soup), ribollita (a rustic vegetable and bread stew), and bistecca alla fiorentina (Florentine steak), all of which are designed to complement the bold flavors of Chianti wines. For those who want to deepen their culinary experience, some day tours from Florence include cooking classes where you can learn to prepare authentic Tuscan dishes. These hands-on experiences are typically led by local chefs and provide a wonderful opportunity to learn about the region's food culture while enjoying the fruits of your labor. The cost of a cooking class usually starts at around 80 euros per person and includes a meal paired with local wines, making it a memorable and enriching addition to your day trip.

Expect the Unexpected: While the vineyards and villages are the star attractions, Chianti is also home to an array of natural wonders that make the journey even more special. As you explore the countryside, you may come across hidden gems such as the stunning Castello di Brolio, a historic castle surrounded by beautiful gardens and vineyards. For nature lovers, Chianti offers hiking and biking trails that wind through forests, olive groves, and vineyards, providing an intimate look at the region's diverse landscapes. These activities can be arranged through local tour operators or on your own, with bike rentals available for around 20 to 40 euros per day. The region's natural beauty is also reflected in its wildlife. Birdwatching is popular, especially around the rippling streams and the dense forests of the Chianti Hills. As you enjoy a peaceful moment surrounded by nature, you'll be reminded of the unhurried pace of life in Chianti – a refreshing contrast to the fast-moving world outside.

6.4 Cinque Terre

A day trip from Florence to Cinque Terre offers an enchanting escape into one of the most picturesque regions of Italy. The Cinque Terre, a collection of rugged coastal villages, is renowned for its dramatic cliffs, colorful houses, and crystal-clear waters. Situated along the Ligurian coastline, this UNESCO World Heritage site invites visitors to immerse themselves in its natural beauty, rich history, and vibrant local culture. While the distance from Florence to Cinque Terre may seem like a challenge, the journey is well worth the effort, whether by train, private car, or organized tour. Here's a detailed guide on what to expect and the best ways to make the most of your day trip to Cinque Terre from Florence.

The Journey to Cinque Terre: The journey from Florence to Cinque Terre spans about 170 kilometers (roughly 105 miles), making it a feasible yet fulfilling excursion. The most common and practical option for travelers is by train, as it offers a straightforward and scenic route, with trains departing regularly from Florence's main station, Santa Maria Novella. The train ride to La Spezia, the gateway to Cinque Terre, typically takes around 2.5 hours. From La Spezia, visitors can switch to the regional trains that connect the five villages, with travel times between the villages ranging from 10 to 20 minutes. A round-trip train ticket from Florence to La Spezia costs approximately 20 to 30 euros, depending on the time of booking and class of service. Once in La Spezia, the Cinque Terre Card, which offers unlimited train travel between the villages for the day, costs around 16 euros, providing a convenient and flexible way to explore the area. For those who prefer a more luxurious or private experience, renting a car or booking a private transfer is another option. The drive from Florence to Cinque Terre typically takes about 2.5 to 3 hours, depending on traffic conditions, and offers the opportunity to enjoy the stunning Tuscan and Ligurian landscapes along the way. However, driving in Cinque Terre can be challenging due to narrow, winding roads and limited parking, especially in the summer months.

The Trails of Cinque Terre: Cinque Terre is also a haven for hikers, and a day trip from Florence offers the perfect opportunity to explore the rugged landscape on foot. The Cinque Terre National Park is crisscrossed with a network of well-marked trails, many of which connect the villages, allowing visitors to experience the dramatic beauty of the coastline up close. The most famous of these is the Sentiero Azzurro, or Blue Trail, which offers panoramic views of the villages and the sea. This trail stretches for about 12 kilometers, connecting all five villages, though some sections may be closed during the summer months due to rockslides or maintenance. The trail is moderately challenging, with sections of steep inclines and narrow paths, but the effort is well worth it. The views from the top are truly mesmerizing, with the villages sprawling below and the Mediterranean stretching endlessly to the horizon. For those looking for a less strenuous hike, there are other trails that offer equally beautiful scenery without the intense uphill climbs. Regardless of which route you take, the experience of walking through the terraced vineyards, olive groves, and lush hillsides, all while breathing in the fresh sea air, is an unforgettable part of any Cinque Terre visit.

CHAPTER 7
ART, ARCHITECTURE, AND HISTORY

7.1 Renaissance Art and Architecture

Florence stands as an unparalleled testament to the Renaissance era. It was during the 14th, 15th, and 16th centuries that Florence blossomed into the cradle of artistic and architectural achievements that would forever change the course of Western civilization. To truly understand the Renaissance art and architecture of Florence is to uncover the depths of its rich cultural background, steeped in the complex interplay of politics, religion, and humanism. This city, filled with masterpieces at every corner, invites visitors to journey through time, where every painting, every sculpture, and every building is a monument to the transformative power of creativity. The origins of Renaissance art and architecture in Florence are deeply intertwined with the city's history and the intellectual movement of humanism. At the heart of the movement was the rediscovery of classical antiquity. Florence, situated in the region of Tuscany, was a center of commerce and trade, drawing scholars, artists, and thinkers from all corners of Europe. The powerful Medici family, who ruled Florence during much of this period, were patrons of the arts, providing the financial support necessary for artists to experiment and innovate. The Medici's influence, both politically and financially, helped to establish Florence as the center of artistic production during the Renaissance.

The cultural climate of Florence in the 14th and 15th centuries was charged with an intense interest in rediscovering the ideas of ancient Greece and Rome. The city's scholars began to revive classical philosophy, science, and art, and this intellectual movement created a foundation for the new wave of artistic expression that followed. The humanist ideals of this period placed emphasis on the individual, the beauty of nature, and the study of classical texts. Artists like Leonardo da Vinci, Sandro Botticelli, and Michelangelo were able to push the boundaries of art, producing works that reflected the complexities of human experience, emotion, and beauty. Florence became the epicenter of this cultural revolution, where the works of these great masters continue to inspire awe and admiration. The architectural achievements of the Renaissance in Florence are as significant as its art. The city's skyline is dominated by the iconic dome of the Cathedral of Santa Maria del Fiore, a masterpiece of engineering and design by Filippo Brunelleschi. The cathedral, with its stunning red-tiled dome, was built to reflect the grandeur of God's creation, and its construction required an innovative solution to a difficult architectural problem. The challenge of constructing such a massive dome over the cathedral's central nave had never been faced before, and Brunelleschi's ingenious use of double-shell construction, along with a herringbone brick pattern, made it possible. The dome remains an architectural marvel to this day, symbolizing the Renaissance's ability to blend art, science, and innovation.

Florence's churches, palaces, and public spaces are filled with other remarkable examples of Renaissance architecture. The Pitti Palace, once home to the powerful Medici family, stands as a testament to the grandeur of the Renaissance period. The Palazzo Vecchio, the political heart of Florence, is another monumental structure that reflects the city's wealth and power during this time. Its imposing façade and the massive Arnolfo Tower were designed to convey authority and strength, while the interior chambers, including the grand Hall of the Five Hundred, showcase the sumptuous tastes of the ruling elite. In addition to its architecture, Florence's streets are lined with some of the world's most famous museums and galleries, housing some of the finest collections of art. The Uffizi Gallery, located along the Arno River, is home to an incredible array of Renaissance paintings, including works by Botticelli, Titian, and Raphael. The Accademia Gallery, another essential stop for art lovers, houses Michelangelo's iconic statue of David, a symbol of human strength and beauty. Walking through the halls of these museums is akin to stepping into the past, where each brushstroke and marble carving tells the story of Florence's profound impact on the world.

The Renaissance in Florence was not merely an artistic movement; it was a cultural awakening that transformed the very fabric of society. It was a time when intellectuals, artists, and architects looked to the past to create a future filled with beauty, order, and meaning. The city's art and architecture reflect this pursuit of perfection, capturing the essence of human potential and the divine. Florence was the stage upon which these masterpieces were created, and even today, the city stands as a living museum, where visitors can experience firsthand the incredible achievements of this golden age. Florence's Renaissance art and architecture were not simply the products of individual genius but were shaped by the collective spirit of a city that believed in the power of human creativity. The city's beauty and historical significance draw visitors from all over the world, eager to witness the cultural legacy that continues to influence art, architecture, and thought. The Renaissance's profound impact on Florence is something that can be felt in every stone of its buildings, every brushstroke on its canvases, and every sculpture that stands proudly in its squares.

7.2 Medici Family and Their Legacy
The Medici family stands as one of the most influential dynasties in the history of Florence, shaping not only the city's culture but also its art, architecture, and historical trajectory. Their rise from modest origins to unparalleled power is a testament to both their skill and ambition. The family's influence on Florence is deep-rooted and pervasive, stretching from the late Middle Ages into the Renaissance. Their patronage of the arts and their role in fostering an environment of intellectual and artistic flourishing helped Florence become a beacon of culture and creativity in Europe. The Medici family's origins can be traced to the Tuscan town of Mugello, just north of Florence. Giovanni di Bicci de' Medici, the family's patriarch, founded the Medici Bank in the late 14th century, an enterprise that quickly became one of the most powerful financial institutions in Europe. The bank's success laid the foundation for the Medici family's future influence in Florence. The wealth they accumulated was instrumental in enabling them to position themselves as patrons of the arts, a role they would embrace with unrivaled enthusiasm.

As their wealth grew, so did their ambitions. The Medici family's patronage transformed Florence into a cradle of Renaissance art and culture. Florence's landscape still echoes with their legacy. The Medici were instrumental in commissioning works from some of the most renowned artists of the time, such as Leonardo da Vinci, Michelangelo, and Botticelli. The family's patronage was not limited to the fine arts; they also funded the construction of remarkable buildings that continue to define Florence's architectural heritage. The most iconic of these is the Palazzo Medici Riccardi, located on Via Cavour, a stunning example of early Renaissance architecture that was commissioned by Cosimo de' Medici in the 15th century. Its elegant design reflects the family's growing power and their commitment to promoting Florentine culture. Beyond their tangible contributions to Florence's architectural and artistic landscapes, the Medici's political influence shaped the city's history for centuries. Cosimo de' Medici, often referred to as Cosimo the Elder, was not just a banker and patron of the arts, but also a shrewd political figure who secured his family's power through careful alliances and strategic marriages. His successor, Lorenzo de' Medici, known as Lorenzo the Magnificent, was one of the most celebrated figures of the Renaissance. Lorenzo's court was a gathering place for poets, philosophers, and artists, making Florence a hub of intellectual activity that would resonate throughout Europe.

The Medici family's influence was not confined to Florence alone. Their legacy reached beyond the city's borders, having a profound impact on Italy and Europe. The Medici popes, such as Leo X and Clement VII, further solidified the family's power and influence, ensuring that their name was etched into the annals of history. Yet, despite their immense wealth and power, the Medici's rule was not without its challenges. Their political machinations and personal rivalries often stirred unrest, and at times, the family faced threats to their dominance. However, their resilience and ability to navigate the complexities of Renaissance politics allowed them to maintain control over Florence for generations. Visiting Florence today is like stepping into a living museum, where the legacy of the Medici family can be seen in every corner of the city. The Uffizi Gallery, one of the world's greatest art museums, is home to masterpieces that the Medici family once commissioned and collected. The Boboli Gardens, an exquisite example of Renaissance landscaping, were developed for the Medici family and continue to offer a peaceful respite for visitors. The Church of San Lorenzo, a Medici family chapel, is a stunning example of Renaissance architecture, with works by Donatello and Michelangelo.

Florence's streets and buildings still bear the marks of the Medici's taste and vision. Each visit to the city reveals something new about this family's lasting impact, making Florence not just a city, but a living testament to the artistic and political brilliance of the Medici. This city, with its rich history, art, and architecture, continues to captivate those who seek to understand the evolution of Western civilization. It invites curiosity, inspiring travelers to explore deeper into its alleys, palaces, and churches, where the echoes of the Medici's influence can still be felt. Florence, through the Medici family, remains an essential destination for those seeking to immerse themselves in the heart of the Renaissance.

7.3 Historical Landmarks and Monuments

A journey through Florence is not just a tour through a city—it is a deep dive into the heart of the Italian Renaissance. The origins of Florence as a cultural hub stretch back to Roman times, but it was during the medieval and Renaissance periods that it truly flourished, becoming a beacon of art, architecture, and intellectual achievement. The cultural background of Florence, particularly its role in shaping Western civilization, cannot be overstated. It was here that thinkers, artists, and scientists such as Leonardo da Vinci, Michelangelo, and Galileo found inspiration, pushing the boundaries of creativity and knowledge. Florence was a place where genius was nurtured and celebrated, creating a legacy that continues to resonate today. As you explore the historical landmarks and monuments of Florence, each site becomes a portal into the city's storied past. The Florence Cathedral, or Duomo, stands proudly at the heart of the city. Its imposing dome, designed by Filippo Brunelleschi, is one of the most iconic architectural feats in the world. The Cathedral, located in Piazza del Duomo, has been an enduring symbol of Florence's religious and cultural significance for centuries. It represents not just an architectural achievement, but also the aspiration of the people of Florence to reach new heights in art, science, and spirituality. The surrounding area, with its medieval streets and churches, is a living testament to the devotion and ambition of those who sought to make Florence the center of the world.

A short walk from the Duomo, the Uffizi Gallery stands as one of the most important art museums in the world. The Uffizi was originally designed by Giorgio Vasari as the offices of Florentine magistrates, hence the name "Uffizi," meaning "offices." Over time, it was transformed into a repository of priceless art, housing works by masters such as Botticelli, Raphael, and Titian. The collection spans centuries, offering visitors a chance to witness the evolution of European art, from the early Renaissance to the Baroque period. But beyond its famous artworks, the Uffizi is also an architectural masterpiece, with its grand halls and windows that open to stunning views of the city. It embodies the Renaissance ideals of beauty, harmony, and proportion, inviting visitors to contemplate both art and the environment that gave birth to such greatness.

Florence is also home to the Ponte Vecchio, a bridge that has crossed the Arno River since Roman times. The Ponte Vecchio is a symbol of the city's resilience and ingenuity. During the Second World War, it was the only bridge in Florence not destroyed by retreating German soldiers, an act that preserved a vital link to the city's history. Today, the bridge is lined with shops, many of which sell gold and jewelry, a tradition that dates back to the 16th century. The Ponte Vecchio is not just a bridge; it's a living, breathing part of Florence's identity, where commerce, history, and culture converge.

Another monument that reflects the city's rich history is the Palazzo Vecchio, located in the Piazza della Signoria. The Palazzo Vecchio has served many roles over the centuries: as the seat of Florence's government, a military fortress, and even as the residence of the ruling Medici family. Its imposing exterior and vast rooms are a testament to the power and influence the Medici once wielded, while the adjacent Piazza della Signoria has long been a gathering place for the people of Florence. The square is home to a number of significant statues, including a replica of Michelangelo's David, which captures the spirit of Florence as a city that celebrates human achievement and the ideals of classical antiquity. Florence's historical landmarks and monuments are not just static relics of the past; they are vibrant reflections of the city's enduring role as a hub of culture, creativity, and thought. The city's profound connection to the Renaissance has left an indelible mark on its identity, one that continues to inspire and fascinate visitors from all over the world. As you walk through the streets of Florence, you are not merely observing history—you are stepping into it, becoming part of a living story that spans centuries.

While Florence's artistic and architectural treasures are undoubtedly remarkable, they also serve as a reminder of the universal desire to create and leave a lasting legacy. The city's remarkable preservation of its past, coupled with its continued commitment to innovation and exploration, makes it a destination that speaks to the heart and soul. Florence offers a timeless experience that draws travelers from around the globe, urging them to experience its beauty, history, and culture firsthand. Just as Florence itself was shaped by the visions of great minds, so too does it continue to shape those who visit, inspiring them to reflect on their own place in the story of human achievement. And so, while Florence may be known as the cradle of the Renaissance, it is also a city that invites you to explore the depths of your own curiosity, to immerse yourself in its rich history, and to discover the artistic and architectural marvels that make it one of the most compelling cities in the world. For those who seek to understand the heart of

Italy, Florence is a journey that is impossible to resist. And, just like Florence, Zanzibar too, with its rich blend of history, culture, and beauty, promises to be a destination that will stir the soul and leave you yearning for more.

7.4 Museums and Galleries

Florence is a city that stands as a testament to the marriage of art, architecture, and history. Known as the birthplace of the Renaissance, its museums and galleries are more than just repositories of art; they are the living essence of a cultural movement that changed the course of Western civilization. Every piece of art, every sculpture, and every fresco in these institutions tells the story of a city that was once the beating heart of Europe's artistic and intellectual awakening. The roots of Florence's artistic legacy stretch back to the early medieval period, but it was during the 14th and 15th centuries, under the influence of wealthy families like the Medici, that the city blossomed into a hub of creativity. The Medici family's patronage attracted the greatest minds of the era, including Leonardo da Vinci, Michelangelo, and Botticelli. Their presence in the city, and the funding they provided, allowed artists to experiment with new techniques and philosophies that would come to define the Renaissance. One of the city's most iconic cultural institutions is the Uffizi Gallery, located along the banks of the Arno River. Built in the mid-16th century by Giorgio Vasari for Francesco I de' Medici, the Uffizi originally served as an office building for Florentine magistrates. Over time, however, it transformed into one of the world's most famous art museums, home to works by da Vinci, Titian, and Caravaggio, among others. As you walk through the gallery's corridors, you are transported back in time, surrounded by masterpieces that were once part of the private collections of the ruling family. The Uffizi offers more than just a glimpse into the minds of great artists; it immerses visitors in the cultural climate of Florence during its golden age.

Another significant venue is the Accademia Gallery, where Michelangelo's iconic sculpture David stands as the centerpiece. This work, perhaps the most famous sculpture in the world, was commissioned by the city in 1501 and has come to symbolize the strength and beauty of the Florentine Republic. The gallery houses other works by Michelangelo, as well as pieces from the late medieval and Renaissance periods, providing a comprehensive view of Florence's artistic evolution. Beyond these well-known institutions, Florence's museums also hold smaller gems that speak volumes about the city's layered history. The Bargello Museum, housed in a former 13th-century prison, is home to an outstanding collection of Renaissance sculptures, including works by

Donatello and Verrocchio. Its quiet, less-crowded atmosphere offers a more intimate experience, allowing visitors to appreciate the intricate details and stories behind each piece. Florence's cultural heritage extends beyond its museums. The city itself is an open-air gallery, with its churches, palaces, and squares serving as living canvases. The Florence Cathedral, with its stunning dome designed by Brunelleschi, stands as a masterpiece of Renaissance architecture. As you stand in its shadow, you can almost hear the whispers of architects and engineers who pushed the boundaries of design, defying the conventions of their time.

The origins of Florence's artistic prominence lie not just in the genius of its artists but in the collective spirit of a city that valued education, creativity, and human potential. Florence became a center for intellectual discourse, attracting scholars from across Europe. The city's commitment to preserving the classical past while embracing innovation allowed it to forge a path that would influence generations of artists, architects, and thinkers. It is this rich cultural history that makes Florence a must-visit destination for anyone interested in art, architecture, and history. The city invites you to walk in the footsteps of legends, to experience the art that changed the world, and to understand the deep connection between the people of Florence and their artistic heritage. Whether you are wandering the halls of the Uffizi, admiring the sculptures of the Accademia, or simply taking in the beauty of the city's streets, Florence offers a journey through time that is as intellectually enriching as it is emotionally stirring. This city, where the past and present blend so seamlessly, continues to be a place of wonder and inspiration for those who seek to understand the transformative power of art and culture.

7.5 Street Art and Contemporary Culture

Florence is often thought of as a place where time stands still, frozen in the elegance of its ancient buildings and masterful artwork. However, beneath the surface of its historical landmarks lies a contemporary culture that thrives through unexpected and vibrant expressions of creativity. In recent years, street art has found a unique space in Florence, weaving itself into the city's fabric of classical architecture, where the old and the new interact in fascinating and sometimes provocative ways. This urban art form not only provides a modern contrast to the city's traditional cultural identity but also offers a glimpse into the voices of today's artists, reflecting global trends and local stories. Florence's street art scene is not just an accident of modern urban life but rather a reflection of a deeper cultural movement. The roots of contemporary street art in the city are intertwined with its long history of artistic innovation. Florence has always been a hub of creativity, from the groundbreaking work of Michelangelo to the vivid frescoes of the Medici chapels. Today, this heritage has evolved, and the walls of Florence now serve as canvases for a new generation of artists. They use their art to engage with the city's cultural pulse, creating works that challenge the boundaries of tradition and make a statement about the present world.

The influence of street art in Florence cannot be separated from the global movements that have shaped it. Italy has been a key player in the evolution of contemporary art, and Florence is no exception. The 21st century brought with it a surge of international street artists who chose to make Florence their home, leaving behind works that speak both to their personal experiences and to universal themes. The city, though traditionally conservative in its approach to art and culture, has gradually come to accept these new forms of artistic expression, creating an exciting tension between the past and the present. Among the most famous locations to see street art in Florence are the lesser-explored streets away from the crowds of the Uffizi Gallery or the Ponte Vecchio. One of the most notable areas is the district of San Frediano, located in the Oltrarno neighborhood. Known for its bohemian vibe, this area is home to murals and installations by renowned local and international artists. The walls here are often transformed into large-scale canvases that depict everything from political statements to personal reflections, and they have become a point of pride for the locals. San Frediano is a part of Florence that feels alive, where the city's traditional spirit meets the energy of youth and rebellion, much like the contemporary art scene itself. But it's not just in the back streets where street art can be found. Florence's historic center, though largely protected due to its UNESCO World Heritage status, has embraced the culture in subtle ways. Areas near the University of Florence and the Santa Croce district showcase a mix of street art, which often reflects the city's blend of intellectual and artistic pursuits. Here, street art takes on a more experimental form, merging graffiti, stencils, and even installations that reflect Florence's academic and cultural undercurrents. In this city, ancient history does not just meet modern art; it becomes a part of it, transforming the cityscape into a dialogue between eras.

One cannot visit Florence without acknowledging its rich history in art and architecture, yet today, this history is not solely defined by the works of the past. The cultural landscape is constantly evolving, and street art is one of the most exciting ways in which this evolution unfolds. This blend of old and new creates a tension that adds complexity to Florence's identity, making it a city that invites visitors to explore not just the art of the Renaissance but also the art of the present. The conversation between the walls of Florence and the artists who mark them is ongoing, and each mural or piece of street art tells a new chapter in the city's history. As a visitor, walking through Florence and discovering its street art can be a revelatory experience. It challenges preconceived notions about the city and invites you to think differently about its culture. These artworks do not just adorn the city's walls—they provoke thought, engage with global conversations, and offer a fresh perspective on a place that is often viewed solely through the lens of its past. The street art in Florence represents more than just artistic defiance—it is a call to embrace change, to understand the present, and to appreciate the city's dynamic blend of history and modernity.

CHAPTER 8
FOOD AND WINE

8.1 Traditional Tuscan Cuisine

Florence is a city rich in history, art, and culture. However, it is perhaps best known for its exceptional cuisine, which reflects the agricultural bounty of the Tuscan region. Traditional Tuscan dishes are often hearty, simple, and made with the freshest ingredients, providing a true taste of the region's rustic charm. From rich stews to delicate pastas and flavorful meats, the food of Florence tells the story of the land and its people. For visitors to Florence, understanding and experiencing the local culinary heritage is an essential part of the journey.

Bistecca alla Fiorentina: A visit to Florence would not be complete without sampling its most famous dish, Bistecca alla Fiorentina. This large, T-bone steak is sourced from the Chianina breed of cattle, one of the oldest and most prestigious in Italy. Typically cooked rare to medium-rare, the steak is grilled over an open flame, seasoned simply with salt, pepper, and olive oil, and served with a squeeze of fresh lemon. The size of the steak is often impressive, making it an ideal dish for sharing. This beloved dish can be found at many traditional trattorias and steakhouses across Florence, with notable spots including Trattoria

Sostanza and Il Latini. The price for Bistecca alla Fiorentina generally starts at around €25 per kilogram, with a typical serving weighing between 1 to 2 kilograms. Visitors should note that the price can vary depending on the establishment and the quality of the meat, but the experience is worth every euro. To fully enjoy Bistecca alla Fiorentina, it is recommended to pair it with a glass of Chianti wine, which complements the richness of the meat beautifully.

Ribollita: Ribollita is one of Tuscany's most beloved comfort foods, especially during the colder months. This traditional vegetable and bread soup is made from simple, humble ingredients, including cannellini beans, kale, onions, carrots, potatoes, and day-old bread. The soup is simmered slowly to allow the flavors to meld together, and it is often served with a drizzle of extra virgin olive oil. Ribollita's name, meaning "reboiled," comes from the practice of reheating the soup over several days, which only enhances its depth of flavor. Ribollita can be found at many trattorias in Florence, particularly in places like Trattoria Mario and La Giostra. Typically, a bowl of Ribollita costs between €10 to €15, depending on the location. For visitors, this dish offers a taste of the Tuscan tradition of using humble ingredients to create something hearty and delicious. It is the perfect choice for those looking to experience a true local meal that has stood the test of time.

Lampredotto: For those seeking an authentic street food experience in Florence, Lampredotto is an essential treat. This flavorful sandwich is made from the fourth stomach of a cow, slow-cooked in a rich broth with herbs and vegetables, then served on a soft bun. The dish is often garnished with fresh salsa verde (a tangy green sauce) and sometimes hot chili sauce for an added kick. Lampredotto is beloved by locals, and it's a popular snack among Florentines during lunch hours. Visitors can find Lampredotto served by street vendors and in casual eateries around Florence, particularly near the San Lorenzo Market and Piazza del Mercato Centrale. A Lampredotto sandwich typically costs around €5 to €7, making it an affordable and flavorful option for those wishing to dive deeper into the local culinary culture. While this dish may sound unusual to some, it offers a unique and authentic taste of Florentine street food and is a must-try for any adventurous eater.

Pappardelle al Cinghiale: Pappardelle al Cinghiale is a rich and savory dish that showcases the wild flavors of Tuscany. Pappardelle, a wide and flat pasta, is paired with a slow-cooked wild boar ragu that is made with tomatoes, red wine, and a blend of herbs. The resulting sauce is rich, slightly gamey, and incredibly flavorful, with the tender boar meat complementing the broad, hearty pasta perfectly. This dish is a true reflection of the Tuscan countryside, where wild boar hunting is a centuries-old tradition. Pappardelle al Cinghiale is typically served in many of Florence's traditional restaurants, such as Trattoria 13 Gobbi and Osteria del Cinghiale Bianco. The price of this dish usually ranges from €12 to €18, depending on the restaurant and the quality of the ingredients. Visitors should take their time savoring this dish, as it captures the essence of Tuscan rural life and offers a unique culinary experience.

Cantucci e Vin Santo: No Tuscan meal is complete without a sweet ending, and Cantucci e Vin Santo is the perfect dessert to cap off a meal. Cantucci are almond biscuits that are crisp and crunchy, often dipped into a glass of Vin Santo, a sweet dessert wine. The tradition of dipping the cantucci into Vin Santo goes back centuries, and the combination of the crunchy biscuits with the smooth, rich wine creates a delightful balance of textures and flavors. Cantucci e Vin Santo is typically served in the final course at many trattorias and osterias in Florence, and it is also sold at local bakeries and cafes. A small serving of Cantucci with a glass of Vin Santo generally costs between €8 to €12. Visitors should not miss this iconic Tuscan treat, as it provides a sweet conclusion to an authentic Florentine dining experience, allowing them to savor the flavors of Tuscany in their purest form.

8.2 Wine Tasting and Vineyard Tours
Florence offers several wine-tasting experiences and vineyard tours that not only showcase the region's world-class wines but also immerse visitors in the rich cultural and gastronomic heritage of this iconic area. Whether you're a seasoned sommelier or a casual wine lover, these tours and tastings offer something for everyone. Below is a comprehensive exploration of distinguished wine experiences in Florence, each promising an unforgettable encounter with Tuscany's most treasured wines.

Castello di Verrazzano: Located just outside the city center of Florence in the Chianti Classico region, Castello di Verrazzano offers an extraordinary wine-tasting experience. The castle itself, dating back to the 11th century, has a long and storied history in the production of wine, with a focus on Chianti Classico wines made from Sangiovese grapes. Guests are greeted with a guided tour of the castle's vineyards and cellars, where they learn about the meticulous process of wine production, from vine to bottle. The wine-tasting session here is a true indulgence, featuring a variety of the estate's wines, including their famous Chianti Classico and the Riserva, which are complemented by delicious local delicacies such as cured meats, cheeses, and freshly baked bread. The tours are offered in multiple languages and are available in the morning and afternoon. Prices for the tours vary, starting at around €25 per person for a basic tour and tasting, with more elaborate experiences, including lunch and wine pairings, going up to €75 per person. Castello di Verrazzano is open daily from 9:30 AM to 6:30 PM, though visitors are advised to book in advance due to the popularity of this vineyard.

Fattoria di Maiano: Another wonderful option for wine lovers is Fattoria di Maiano, a beautiful estate situated just a few kilometers from the city of Florence, near the picturesque town of Fiesole. This family-owned farm offers a tranquil retreat, set amidst rolling hills covered in olive groves and vineyards. The estate's wines are crafted from traditional Tuscan grape varieties, and visitors have the opportunity to taste a selection of reds, whites, and rosés while enjoying panoramic views of Florence and the surrounding countryside. Fattoria di Maiano specializes in organic wine production, and the tasting experience emphasizes the natural connection between the land and the wines. Guests can sample the estate's signature wines, such as the Chianti Colli Fiorentini, and are often treated to a selection of regional products like olive oil, honey, and artisanal cheeses. A unique feature of the vineyard is its commitment to sustainable farming practices, which is evident in the high-quality, organic wines they produce. The tours typically include a visit to the ancient cellar and the vineyards, where visitors can learn about the estate's biodynamic farming practices. The prices for wine tastings at Fattoria di Maiano range from €20 to €50, depending on the type of experience and the number of wines included. For those seeking a more immersive experience, the estate also offers cooking classes where participants can learn how to prepare traditional Tuscan dishes, paired with wines from the estate. Fattoria di Maiano is open daily from 10:00 AM to 6:00 PM.

Tenuta San Vito: For those looking to explore the Chianti region's hidden gems, Tenuta San Vito is a vineyard and winery that offers a truly intimate and personal experience. Located in the hills of Greve in Chianti, about 30 minutes from Florence, Tenuta San Vito is a small, family-run estate that specializes in producing high-quality Chianti Classico wines. The estate's wines are produced using both traditional methods and modern techniques, ensuring that the character of the region shines through in every bottle. The wine tour at Tenuta San Vito is a more intimate affair compared to larger vineyards, with small groups enjoying a relaxed, in-depth look at the winemaking process. The tasting session here is particularly memorable as visitors get to savor the estate's exceptional reds, including Chianti Classico, while being served a variety of local foods such as pecorino cheese, prosciutto, and olive oil. One of the most unique features of this vineyard is its close connection to the land, with an emphasis on small-scale, sustainable farming that ensures high-quality production. Visitors can opt for a range of tasting experiences, with prices starting from €20 for a basic tasting to around €50 for a more premium experience with food pairings. The vineyard is open daily from 10:00 AM to 5:00 PM, but advance booking is highly recommended, as the estate prefers to keep tours small and personalized.

Villa Vignamaggio: If you are looking for a wine-tasting experience that combines history, beauty, and superb wines, then Villa Vignamaggio should be at the top of your list. Situated in the heart of the Chianti region, this historic villa was once the birthplace of Lisa Gherardini, the woman who is famously believed to be the subject of Leonardo da Vinci's "Mona Lisa." Today, the estate is renowned for its production of fine wines, including Chianti Classico, and offers one of the most scenic and historic wine-tasting experiences in Tuscany. Visitors to Villa Vignamaggio are treated to a guided tour of the vineyard, followed by a wine-tasting session in the villa's charming tasting room. The experience is often complemented with light snacks, including local cheeses, cured meats, and freshly baked bread. Villa Vignamaggio's wines are crafted with great care, and the estate offers a wide variety of reds, whites, and rosés for tasting. The unique feature of this estate is its deep historical roots, and guests are often fascinated by the connection between the wines and the history of the villa. The cost for a wine-tasting tour at Villa Vignamaggio ranges from €20 to €60, depending on the experience chosen. Guests can enjoy a light tasting or opt for a more extensive tour, including a gourmet meal paired with wines from the estate. The villa is open every day from 9:30 AM to 6:00 PM, and reservations are recommended to ensure availability.

Podere il Carnasciale: For those who appreciate the artistry of winemaking, Podere il Carnasciale is a boutique winery that offers an exclusive and refined wine-tasting experience. Situated in the hills of the Chianti Montalbano area, just outside Florence, Podere il Carnasciale is known for producing some of the finest small-batch wines in the region. The winery's signature wine, the "Carnasciale," is a rare blend of Cabernet Franc and Merlot, creating a rich, full-bodied wine that has gained recognition among wine connoisseurs. The tour at Podere il Carnasciale is a more personal and intimate experience, allowing guests to explore the winery's production methods and discover the story behind their unique wines. The wine tasting is typically held in the estate's beautiful outdoor space, offering sweeping views of the Tuscan hills. Alongside the wine, guests are treated to a selection of locally produced olive oils, cheeses, and meats, perfectly paired with the wines. The estate's commitment to sustainable practices and artisanal wine production is evident in every detail of the tour. Wine tastings at Podere il Carnasciale start at €35 per person and can go up to €80 for a more premium experience with additional pairings and a private tour. The estate is open by appointment only, and visitors are encouraged to book in advance to ensure a spot. Podere il Carnasciale is open year-round, though the best time to visit is during the harvest season when the vineyard is brimming with activity and the wines are at their freshest.

8.3 Local Markets and Food Shopping

The local markets of this vibrant Italian city are a reflection of its traditions, where fresh produce, artisanal products, and local specialties come together to create an authentic food experience. These markets are not just places to shop but are cultural hubs where locals and visitors alike can immerse themselves in the flavors of Tuscany. From bustling food stalls to quiet corners of artisanal delights, Florence's markets offer a unique journey for any food lover. Here are the most beloved local markets in Florence, each offering a distinct flavor of the city.

Mercato Centrale: Located in the San Lorenzo district, Mercato Centrale is one of the most iconic markets in Florence, steeped in history and bursting with fresh ingredients. The market is housed in a grand 19th-century building with a stunning wrought-iron structure, and it's a must-visit for any foodie in the city. In its ground floor, traditional market stalls line the space, offering an array of fresh produce, meats, cheeses, and seafood. The selection of seasonal fruits and vegetables is abundant, with many local Tuscan varieties that are difficult to find elsewhere. Visitors can also find cured meats like prosciutto and salami, as well as artisanal cheeses such as pecorino and mozzarella di bufala. The second floor of the Mercato Centrale is a modern food court that features a variety of gourmet eateries, offering everything from traditional Tuscan street food to refined Italian dishes. Here, you can savor an authentic lampredotto sandwich, a Florentine specialty made from the slow-cooked stomach of a cow, served on a soft roll with salsa verde. The market is also home to several wine bars, where visitors can sample local wines, such as Chianti and Brunello di Montalcino.

The prices are reasonable, with fresh produce starting from as little as a few euros, and a meal in the food court ranging from 10 to 20 euros, depending on your choice. Mercato Centrale is open every day from 8:00 AM to midnight, with the food stalls operating until 3:00 PM. Whether you're looking to buy ingredients for your next meal or indulge in a delicious lunch, Mercato Centrale is a great place to experience the heart of Florence's food culture.

Mercato di Sant'Ambrogio: A short walk from the city center, Mercato di Sant'Ambrogio offers a more local and laid-back atmosphere compared to Mercato Centrale. This market is a hidden gem, favored by Florentines for its authenticity and charm. Open since the early 1900s, the market has remained true to its roots, providing locals with fresh, high-quality produce at affordable prices. The market's interior is divided into various sections, with an abundance of fruit, vegetables, and herbs that reflect the agricultural diversity of Tuscany. Vendors sell local specialties like Tuscan bread, fresh pasta, and fragrant olive oils. One of the standout features of Mercato di Sant'Ambrogio is its emphasis on regional products. You can find a selection of meats from local butchers, including Tuscan sausages and wild boar, as well as delicious fresh cheeses from nearby dairies. The market also has a small selection of specialty stores where you can find homemade jams, pickles, and other pantry essentials, often made with traditional methods passed down through generations. Prices at Sant'Ambrogio are more affordable than in the city center, with fresh produce available for as little as 2 to 3 euros per kilo. You can expect to spend around 5 to 15 euros on a meal at one of the local cafes or trattorias surrounding the market. Mercato di Sant'Ambrogio operates Monday to Saturday, from 7:00 AM to 3:00 PM, making it a great spot for an early morning visit.

Mercato delle Pulci: For those seeking a more eclectic experience, Mercato delle Pulci, located near Piazza dei Ciompi, is a Florence institution that blends vintage treasures with food. This market, best known for its antiques and second-hand goods, also boasts a number of food stalls that offer unique, locally sourced products. While wandering through the aisles of vintage furniture and old books, visitors will encounter vendors selling cured meats, cheeses, and an assortment of local wines. It's a great place to discover artisanal food products that you won't find in other markets, like truffle-infused oils and locally made pasta. In addition to its culinary offerings, Mercato delle Pulci provides a more intimate, off-the-beaten-path atmosphere. The prices here vary depending on what you're purchasing, but it's possible to find a variety of fresh produce for around 3 to 6 euros, while a bottle of local wine can cost anywhere from 5 to 20 euros. If you're looking for a unique gift or souvenir, you can pick up a handmade pasta set or a jar of homemade sauce to take home. The market is open daily from 9:00 AM to 7:00 PM, with the busiest days being weekends.

Mercato di San Lorenzo: The Mercato di San Lorenzo is another popular market that combines history with local flavors. Located just behind the famous Basilica di San Lorenzo, this market has been a part of Florence's food scene for centuries, dating back to the 1400s. Though the exterior of the market building is quite modern, the inside retains its traditional charm, with a variety of food stalls offering fresh meats, fish, and cheeses. Many of the vendors here specialize in Tuscan meats like bistecca alla fiorentina (Florentine steak), a must-try for any meat lover. One of the most famous aspects of this market is its focus on high-quality, sustainable products. You'll find small-scale producers selling fresh vegetables, hand-made pasta, and local honey. Prices here are generally in line with other markets in the city, with fresh produce starting around 3 euros per kilo, and specialty meats ranging from 10 to 30 euros per kilogram. For visitors, the market is an excellent place to pick up ingredients for a homemade Italian meal or to enjoy a traditional Florentine lunch at one of the many nearby trattorias. Mercato di San Lorenzo is open every day except Sundays, from 7:00 AM to 2:00 PM, so it's best to visit early in the day for the freshest selection.

La Bottega del Buon Caffè: While not a traditional market, La Bottega del Buon Caffè offers an exceptional food-shopping experience for those looking for high-end, local products. Located along the Arno River, this gourmet food store specializes in artisanal products, including some of the finest olive oils, cured meats, and cheeses that Tuscany has to offer. It is known for its carefully curated selection of local delicacies, many of which are produced in small batches by family-owned farms and food artisans. The store also offers a selection of fine wines, including rare bottles from the region's prestigious wineries. For those seeking a unique culinary experience, La Bottega del Buon Caffè provides gourmet gift baskets, cooking classes, and personalized tours of local farms, making it an excellent stop for food lovers looking to dive deeper into Tuscan cuisine. Prices here tend to be higher than in the traditional markets, with specialty items like aged balsamic vinegar or truffle-infused oil costing upwards of 20 euros. The store is open daily from 10:00 AM to 7:00 PM, providing ample time to explore the diverse selection of gourmet products on offer.

8.4 Cooking Classes and Workshops

Florence offers an array of immersive cooking classes and workshops that allow visitors to experience the authentic flavors of Tuscany. These experiences offer much more than just a lesson in cooking; they are a journey into the heart of Italian culture, traditions, and history. From preparing classic Italian pasta to learning the art of making regional desserts, each class offers something unique. Below are the top cooking experiences in Florence, each providing an unforgettable opportunity to learn, taste, and enjoy the delights of Tuscan cuisine.

Tuscan Cooking Class at In Tavola: Located in the heart of Florence, In Tavola offers an intimate and hands-on cooking class that takes participants through the essential elements of Tuscan cuisine. Situated just a short walk from Piazza della Repubblica, this workshop focuses on traditional Italian dishes, with a heavy emphasis on the regional flavors of Tuscany. In Tavola offers a wide variety of classes, ranging from fresh pasta making to creating rustic Tuscan breads and sauces. Guests learn to prepare dishes such as ribollita (a traditional Tuscan soup), pappardelle with wild boar ragu, and cantucci, the classic almond biscuits served with Vin Santo. Classes typically last around four hours, and at the end of the session, guests get to enjoy their meal paired with local wines. The price of the class is approximately €90 per person, which includes the full meal, drinks, and a recipe booklet to take home. The classes are conducted in a cozy, professional kitchen with small groups, ensuring personalized attention. In Tavola opens its doors daily from 9:00 AM until 6:00 PM, and it is recommended to book ahead, especially during the busy tourist seasons.

La Cucina di Olga: For those seeking a more immersive, personal experience, La Cucina di Olga offers small, private cooking workshops in a family-like setting. Olga, a passionate local chef, invites guests into her kitchen located just outside the center of Florence. The classes here are deeply rooted in Italian family traditions, where participants get to learn not only how to cook but also the stories behind each dish. The classes are usually held in the morning, starting at 9:30 AM, and last approximately 5 hours. Dishes taught include homemade pasta, Tuscan meats, and decadent desserts like tiramisu or panna cotta. Olga's kitchen is filled with rustic charm, and the experience feels much like a visit to a friend's home. The workshop includes a tour of the local markets, where guests will pick fresh ingredients for the day's meal. After cooking, a communal lunch is served, complete with wines from the Chianti region. Prices for the class are around €110 per person, which includes the market tour, cooking lesson, and lunch. The workshops are available Tuesday through Saturday, and reservations are essential due to the intimate nature of the classes.

Accademia Italiana Cucina: For those interested in a more structured, professional approach to Italian cooking, Accademia Italiana Cucina offers an educational and hands-on cooking experience in the heart of Florence. This well-established culinary school provides a variety of courses that cover both traditional Tuscan cuisine and more modern interpretations of Italian dishes. Classes range from single-day sessions focused on pasta and sauces to multi-day programs designed for serious culinary enthusiasts. At Accademia, you'll be guided by experienced chefs through intricate recipes that bring the essence of Italian cuisine to life. Some popular classes include making fresh pasta, risotto, and traditional Italian antipasti. The school offers both group and private sessions, with a maximum of 12 participants per class to ensure personalized instruction. The prices vary depending on the course length, ranging from €80 for a half-day session to €450 for a week-long intensive. Accademia Italiana Cucina operates Monday to Friday, with classes typically running from 9:00 AM to 3:00 PM. It's an ideal option for those who are serious about mastering the art of Italian cooking.

Florence Cooking Class and Market Tour by Walkabout Florence: For an experience that combines the vibrant atmosphere of Florence's bustling markets with hands-on cooking, Walkabout Florence offers a unique cooking class that begins with a guided tour of the city's famous San Lorenzo Market. This market is one of the best places in Florence to experience local products, and the tour provides a fascinating look at the freshest ingredients that define Tuscan cuisine. After the market visit, participants head to a nearby kitchen where they can start preparing dishes that range from classic pasta to meat-based dishes like Florentine steak. This cooking class is not just about the food; it's about the experience of shopping for the ingredients, learning how to cook them, and then enjoying the meal with fellow travelers. Classes typically last about 4 hours and are priced around €95 per person. The price includes the market tour, cooking class, and a tasting session with wine pairings. Walkabout Florence operates every day from 10:00 AM to 3:00 PM, and it's highly recommended to book in advance, as this hands-on experience tends to fill up quickly.

GustaVino Cooking Class: For those who want to explore the relationship between food and wine in Tuscany, GustaVino offers an exceptional cooking class focused on pairing the best local wines with Tuscan dishes. Located just a short walk from the Arno River, GustaVino provides a unique blend of culinary education and wine tasting. The class focuses on creating a multi-course meal that reflects the local flavors of the region, such as crostini toscani (chicken liver pate), pasta alla chitarra, and a variety of seasonal vegetable dishes. The most intriguing aspect of this class is the wine pairing, where each course is paired with a carefully selected Tuscan wine, including Chianti and Brunello di Montalcino. Participants will gain knowledge not only in cooking but also in wine appreciation, learning how to enhance the flavors of both. Classes typically run for about 3.5 hours, and the price is approximately €90 per person. The class is available daily, with morning sessions starting at 10:00 AM. GustaVino is known for its relaxed and friendly atmosphere, and bookings are essential to ensure a spot in this popular experience.

8.5 Gelato and Coffee Culture

The Italian tradition of coffee and gelato is a cornerstone of Florentine life, and visitors are invited to indulge in these iconic delights. Whether you're sipping an espresso while people-watching in Piazza del Duomo or enjoying a creamy gelato on a warm afternoon, Florence offers a wealth of authentic experiences that are simply not to be missed. Here are the finest spots in Florence where you can explore the best of gelato and coffee culture.

Gelateria dei Neri: Located on Via dei Neri, Gelateria dei Neri is a quintessential stop for gelato lovers seeking a traditional and authentic experience. This renowned gelateria has become a staple in Florence, offering a broad range of flavors made with the finest ingredients. Here, you can expect everything from classic fruit flavors like strawberry and lemon to rich, indulgent options like pistachio and dark chocolate. One of the standout features of Gelateria dei Neri is their commitment to seasonal ingredients, ensuring that the flavors are as fresh as possible. The prices here are reasonable, with a small cone starting at around €2.50, making it an accessible treat for anyone looking to experience the essence of Italian gelato. For those looking to indulge further, a large cone with two scoops will cost around €4.50. What sets Gelateria dei Neri apart is not just its creamy gelato but its friendly and welcoming staff, who take great pride in serving each customer. The shop is open daily from 10:30 AM to midnight, allowing you to satisfy your gelato cravings at nearly any time of day or night.

Caffè Gilli: For a true taste of Florence's coffee culture, a visit to Caffè Gilli is essential. Situated in the heart of the city, right on Piazza della Repubblica, this historic café has been serving some of the finest coffee in Florence since 1733. The elegant setting, with its high ceilings, velvet upholstery, and gilded mirrors, transports you back in time to an era when coffeehouses were the intellectual meeting places of Europe. Today, Caffè Gilli continues to be a hub for both locals and tourists looking to enjoy the ritual of Italian coffee. Caffè Gilli offers a range of coffee options, from the beloved espresso to more elaborate beverages like cappuccinos and macchiatos. The prices here are reflective of the café's upscale atmosphere, with an espresso typically costing around €2, and a cappuccino setting you back about €3.50. In addition to coffee, the café also serves a variety of pastries, sandwiches, and other light fare, perfect for a midday break. The café opens its doors early at 7:30 AM and remains open until 10:00 PM, giving visitors ample opportunity to enjoy its offerings throughout the day.

La Ménagère: La Ménagère, located on Via de' Ginori, is a modern and chic space where coffee and gelato come together with a contemporary flair. The café is housed in a beautifully restored building that combines the rustic charm of Florence with a fresh, modern aesthetic. Known for its innovative menu, La Ménagère serves coffee from some of the best local roasters, offering an impressive selection of blends and single-origin beans. Visitors can enjoy everything from classic espressos to more complex drinks like flat whites and iced coffees. The gelato at La Ménagère is equally impressive. While the café offers some traditional gelato flavors, it also features unique options like salted caramel and matcha, reflecting the café's penchant for experimentation and creativity. The prices are moderate, with coffee ranging from €2 for a simple espresso to €5 for a specialty drink, and gelato cones starting at €3.50. La Ménagère's ambiance is perfect for those looking for a more contemporary coffee experience in Florence, where they can sip their drink surrounded by greenery, artisanal décor, and a cozy atmosphere. The café is open daily from 8:00 AM to 8:00 PM.

Vivoli Gelato: When it comes to classic gelato in Florence, Vivoli is an institution that stands out. Located on Via Isola delle Stinche, this gelateria has been serving locals and tourists since 1930. Known for its rich, creamy textures and authentic flavors, Vivoli offers a taste of Florentine history in every scoop. The gelateria's small but delicious menu features a selection of traditional flavors, including the ever-popular chocolate and hazelnut, as well as more unique offerings like ricotta and fig. Vivoli's gelato is made with high-quality ingredients, and the staff take great pride in ensuring that each serving is a perfect balance of sweetness and creaminess. Prices here are slightly higher than other gelaterias, with a small cone priced at around €3.50, and a large cone with two scoops at about €5. Vivoli's location, just a short walk from the Santa Croce Church, makes it a convenient stop for anyone exploring the city. The gelateria opens from 11:00 AM to 7:00 PM, so visitors can enjoy a refreshing treat during the afternoon or early evening hours.

Ditta Artigianale: Ditta Artigianale, located on Via dei Neri and Via del Corso, is a popular specialty coffee shop that has gained a reputation for its expertly brewed coffees and modern, minimalist décor. This is the place for coffee connoisseurs looking to explore the world of artisanal brews in Florence. Ditta Artigianale serves an array of specialty coffee drinks, from simple espressos to pour-over coffee and flat whites, all made with beans sourced from the best Italian roasters. In addition to its extensive coffee menu, Ditta Artigianale offers a selection of pastries, sandwiches, and light bites to accompany your drink. The café also has a reputation for its innovative approach to coffee, offering cold brews and nitro coffees that are perfect for a hot day. Prices are reasonable for the quality, with espressos starting at around €2.50, and a flat white priced at about €4. Ditta Artigianale is open daily from 8:00 AM to 8:00 PM, making it an ideal spot for a morning coffee or a late afternoon pick-me-up.

CHAPTER 9
PRACTICAL INFORMATION AND TRAVEL RESOURCES

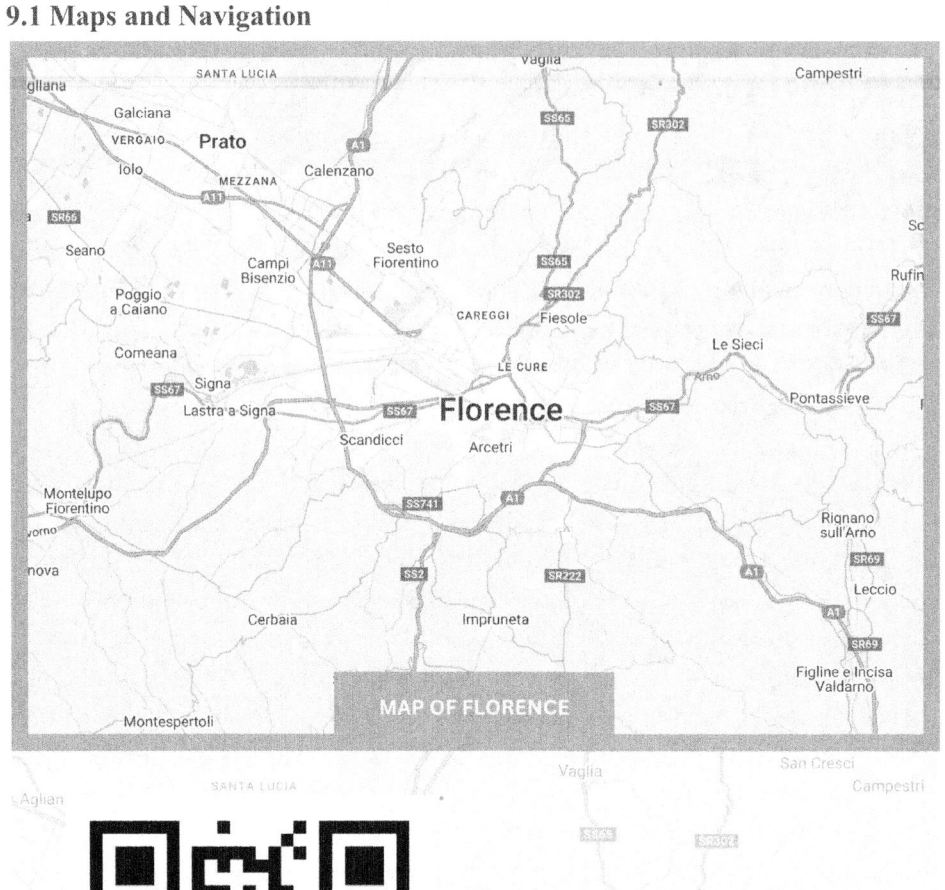

9.1 Maps and Navigation

MAP OF FLORENCE

SCAN THE QR CODE WITH A DEVICE TO VIEW A COMPRHENSIVE AND LARGER MAP OF FLORENCE

113

This guide will help you navigate Florence, focusing on both physical tourist maps and the growing presence of digital maps that make it easier than ever to explore the city.

Exploring Florence with a Tourist Map: A paper map of Florence is an essential tool for any traveler visiting this enchanting city. Most tourist information centers, hotels, and bookshops in Florence offer free or inexpensive paper maps, which are particularly useful for those who prefer a tangible resource to carry with them. These maps are often simple, easy to follow, and specifically designed for tourists. They usually highlight key landmarks such as the Duomo, Ponte Vecchio, the Uffizi Gallery, and other famous attractions. By referring to a physical map, visitors can gain a better understanding of the city's layout, and the scale of the map allows them to plan their routes effectively. Florence's historic center is compact and walkable, making it possible to explore many of the major sights on foot. A tourist map provides helpful information, not just about monuments, but also about nearby restaurants, shops, and hidden gems that may otherwise be overlooked. These maps often feature marked pedestrian paths, which are invaluable for tourists wishing to avoid the bustling main roads and instead enjoy a quieter stroll through Florence's picturesque streets. You can find paper maps in places like the Florence Tourist Information Centers located near the Santa Maria Novella train station or inside the major museums. Many hotels also provide their guests with a map at check-in, so it's always worth asking. You may even come across specialized maps that focus on specific themes, such as art, architecture, or local food tours, adding even more depth to your experience.

Accessing Digital Maps in Florence: As technology continues to evolve, the way we navigate Florence has become increasingly digital. Digital maps have revolutionized the way travelers explore cities, offering unparalleled convenience and interactivity. One of the best things about digital maps is that they can be accessed anytime and anywhere, as long as you have an internet connection or pre-downloaded data. The most widely used digital maps for Florence are offered through popular platforms like Google Maps, Apple Maps, and other navigation apps. These tools provide real-time GPS navigation, enabling you to easily plot your route from one point to another, whether you're heading to the Duomo or exploring the artisan workshops of the Oltrarno district. Google Maps, for example, is particularly beneficial as it offers walking directions, public transport routes, and traffic updates, making it an indispensable companion for tourists. It also highlights points of interest, dining options, and even reviews, helping you make informed decisions about where to go and what to do in Florence. In addition to the major mapping apps, there are several digital resources specifically designed for Florence that can enhance your travel experience. For instance, the Florence Walking Tour app provides guided tours of the city's most important landmarks, offering historical insights and multimedia content. These specialized apps are great for immersing yourself in the rich history of Florence while navigating the streets.

Offline Access to Maps: One of the challenges of using digital maps is the need for an internet connection, which can be costly or unreliable, especially for international travelers. Fortunately, there are ways to access Florence's maps offline, ensuring that you're never lost, even when you're without data. Many mapping apps, including Google Maps, allow users to download specific areas of a city or region for offline use. Before you embark on your journey, you can download a map of Florence, which will enable you to navigate the city seamlessly without requiring constant internet access. Another option for offline navigation is to use digital guidebooks or map apps specifically designed for travelers. These apps often provide downloadable maps and guides, allowing you to access all the essential information without an active internet connection. Some popular apps even include detailed walking tours and recommendations based on your location, so you can explore Florence at your own pace, whether online or offline. For those who prefer a more traditional approach, many downloadable PDF maps are available, which can be stored on your phone or tablet and accessed without any internet connection. These PDFs often mirror the paper maps found at tourist information points and may be available through various travel websites or apps, giving you the flexibility to choose the map format that works best for your needs.

Accessing Florence's Map Through Links and QR Codes: For modern convenience, many printed travel guides, including this book, offer a digital alternative to the paper maps you receive in tourist offices. With just a click on the link or by scanning the QR code provided, you can access a comprehensive, interactive map of Florence directly on your mobile device. This digital map allows you to zoom in on specific areas, search for locations, and plan your visit in real-time. These interactive maps are incredibly helpful, as they can provide more details than the typical paper map. From real-time updates to additional recommendations, digital maps can enhance your visit by helping you make the most of your time in Florence. By scanning the QR code, you can get immediate access to a digital map that is constantly updated, providing the latest information on new attractions, construction projects, or temporary closures.

9.2 Five Days Itinerary

A five-day itinerary is the perfect amount of time to explore the essence of this extraordinary city, whether you are a first-time visitor or a seasoned traveler seeking to immerse yourself in its rich heritage. Each day of this itinerary provides a balance between famous attractions, hidden gems, cultural experiences, and leisure, allowing you to experience Florence at a relaxed and enriching pace.

Day One: Exploring the Historic Center

Your first day in Florence should focus on exploring the iconic sights located in the heart of the city. The day begins at the Piazza del Duomo, where you will find the magnificent Florence Cathedral, Santa Maria del Fiore, which dominates the skyline. Admire the intricate details of the cathedral's facade, but make sure to venture inside to witness the awe-inspiring interior, including the remarkable frescoes on the dome by Giorgio Vasari. For a panoramic view of the city, climb to the top of the cathedral's dome or the nearby Giotto's Campanile. After absorbing the grandeur of the Duomo, take a short walk to the Baptistery of St. John, one of Florence's oldest buildings. Its golden mosaics and the famous Gates of Paradise by Lorenzo Ghiberti are must-sees. As you continue your stroll through the historic center, head towards the Piazza della Signoria, home to the Palazzo Vecchio. This medieval fortress-palace serves as both a museum and the city's town hall, and its ornate interior is a fascinating glimpse into Florence's political past. In the afternoon, take the time to visit the Uffizi Gallery, one of the world's greatest art museums. Located just behind the Palazzo Vecchio, the Uffizi houses works by legendary artists such as Botticelli, Leonardo da Vinci, and Michelangelo. With its vast collection of Renaissance art, it's easy to spend hours marveling at the masterpieces. Finish your day with a leisurely walk along the Arno River, crossing the iconic Ponte Vecchio, and enjoy dinner at one of the many riverside restaurants.

Day Two: Art, Gardens, and Views

On your second day in Florence, delve deeper into the city's rich artistic heritage. Begin by visiting the Galleria dell'Accademia, where you'll find Michelangelo's David. This colossal sculpture is one of the most famous pieces of art in the world, and standing before it, you can truly appreciate its perfection. The museum also houses other works by Michelangelo and Renaissance artists, offering a fascinating glimpse into the artistic evolution of Florence. From there, make your way to the beautiful Boboli Gardens, a short walk from the Pitti Palace. These expansive gardens provide a peaceful escape from the city's hustle and bustle and offer stunning views of Florence. As you wander through the formal gardens, be sure to stop at the Grotta del Buontalenti, a striking grotto designed by the architect Giorgio Vasari. The gardens themselves are an artwork, with fountains, statues, and lush greenery surrounding you. In the afternoon, visit the Pitti Palace, once the home of the powerful Medici family. The palace is now a museum, housing several art collections, including works by Raphael, Titian, and Caravaggio. After exploring the palace's galleries, head to the nearby Bardini Gardens, another picturesque spot that offers one of the best panoramic views of Florence. Here, you can relax and enjoy the beauty of the city from a more serene vantage point, away from the crowds.

Day Three: A Day in the Oltrarno District
Day three takes you to the Oltrarno, the neighborhood located across the Arno River from the historic center. Start by visiting the Basilica di Santo Spirito, a church designed by Brunelleschi, which is often less crowded than Florence's other major churches. Its simple, yet beautiful, design and tranquil atmosphere make it a lovely stop. From here, stroll through the artisan shops and studios that make the Oltrarno so unique. The district is known for its traditional craftsmanship, and you can visit workshops where artisans create leather goods, jewelry, and fine art. Stop for lunch in one of the local trattorias, where you can enjoy traditional Tuscan dishes such as ribollita (a hearty vegetable soup) or bistecca alla fiorentina (Florentine steak). In the afternoon, head to the Palazzo Pitti and explore the Palatine Gallery, which houses an extensive collection of Renaissance art, and then take a walk to the nearby Belvedere Fort for a scenic view of the city. For a peaceful end to your day, visit the nearby Rose Garden (Giardino delle Rose), where you can enjoy beautiful flowers and a quiet space to unwind.

Day Four: Day Trip to the Tuscan Countryside
On your fourth day in Florence, take a day trip into the Tuscan countryside. The region around Florence is renowned for its vineyards, rolling hills, and charming medieval towns. You can take a short bus or train ride to the nearby town of Fiesole, which offers a fantastic view of Florence from its hilltop location. Fiesole is home to ancient Roman ruins, including an amphitheater, and the town's peaceful atmosphere makes it an ideal escape from the busy city. Another

option is to take a wine tour through the Chianti region, one of the most famous wine-growing areas in the world. Several guided tours offer visits to local wineries, where you can taste the region's best wines while enjoying a delicious Tuscan lunch. The rolling vineyards, olive groves, and charming villages make this a perfect day trip to immerse yourself in the beauty of the Tuscan landscape. If you prefer a more active excursion, consider a hike in the surrounding hills of Florence, such as the Fiesole hills or the hiking trails near the town of Settignano. These trails offer incredible views of Florence and provide an opportunity to experience the countryside in a more intimate way.

Day Five: Florence's Lesser-Known Treasures
For your final day in Florence, take the time to explore some of the city's lesser-known treasures. Start by visiting the Museo di San Salvi, a small and intimate museum housed in a former convent. It offers a peaceful environment to enjoy a range of works by Florentine artists, far from the crowds. Another hidden gem is the Museo Horne, a small museum showcasing the private collection of an American art collector. Its eclectic mix of Renaissance and Medieval art, as well as antique furniture, offers an insight into Florence's artistic history beyond the mainstream attractions. Later, wander through the lively San Lorenzo market, where you can shop for souvenirs, local products, and fresh Tuscan ingredients. The nearby Mercato Centrale is also worth a visit for food lovers, as it offers a wide range of local delicacies and street food. As your trip to Florence comes to a close, take a final walk along the Arno River at sunset. The view of the Ponte Vecchio bathed in golden light is the perfect way to bid farewell to this beautiful city, leaving you with unforgettable memories of art, history, and culture.

9.3 Essential Packing List
Whether you're embarking on a short getaway or an extended stay, packing the right items will ensure you enjoy your time in the city to the fullest. Florence's climate, cultural norms, and extensive walking routes all factor into what you'll need to bring along for your journey. With this in mind, planning your packing list carefully can make a significant difference in how comfortable and convenient your visit will be. The following guide provides an extensive and comprehensive packing list, tailored to make your time in Florence seamless and enjoyable.

Clothing for Florence's Seasonal Weather: Florence's climate can vary greatly depending on the time of year, so it's essential to pack clothing suited to the season of your visit. Summers in Florence are hot and dry, often reaching temperatures well into the 30s°C (high 80s°F to 90s°F). Lightweight, breathable clothing is a must for the summer months. Cotton or linen fabrics work well to keep you cool, and comfortable shorts, skirts, and light dresses are suitable for sightseeing during the day. However, evenings can cool off, especially in the later months of summer, so packing a light jacket or sweater is advisable. Autumn and spring in Florence offer more moderate weather, with temperatures ranging from mild to cool, often between 10°C and 20°C (50°F to 70°F). Layering is essential during these months. A light sweater, jacket, and scarves will help adjust to the shifting temperatures throughout the day. The spring also brings occasional rain, so bringing a compact, foldable umbrella is a wise choice. The fall months can also be unpredictable, with occasional rain showers, so having a waterproof jacket is recommended. Winter in Florence is usually cool, with temperatures ranging from 3°C to 12°C (37°F to 54°F). While snow is rare, it does occur, so packing a warm coat or jacket is essential. Along with warm layers, you may want to pack gloves, a scarf, and hats to stay cozy while exploring the city's outdoor sights.

Comfortable Footwear for Exploring the City: Florence is best explored on foot, with much of the city's charm located in its narrow streets, cobblestone alleys, and piazzas. Comfortable walking shoes are perhaps the most important item to include in your packing. A sturdy pair of sneakers or walking shoes is ideal for long days of sightseeing. Be sure that the shoes are broken in before your trip to avoid blisters. If you plan on dining in upscale restaurants or attending special events, you may want to pack a pair of dress shoes or sandals, depending on the season. It's also important to keep in mind the city's cobblestone streets, which can be tricky to navigate with thin heels. Opting for flats, supportive sandals, or sneakers with good soles will make navigating these uneven surfaces much easier. Waterproof shoes can also be a smart choice, especially if you're traveling during the rainy months.

Cultural Considerations and Modesty: Florence, like much of Italy, takes pride in its cultural heritage, and visitors should be mindful of the expectations surrounding dress, particularly when visiting religious sites. While casual clothing is acceptable in most public areas, it's important to note that certain places, such as the Duomo, the Uffizi Gallery, and the churches of Florence, require more modest attire. It is customary to cover shoulders and knees when entering religious sites, so packing a lightweight scarf or shawl to drape over your shoulders can be very helpful.

Accessories for Practicality and Style: A day in Florence often involves long hours of sightseeing, and it's important to pack a bag that is both practical and stylish. A comfortable crossbody bag or a small backpack is ideal for carrying essentials like your phone, wallet, camera, and a water bottle. Consider choosing a bag that is secure, especially if you plan to visit crowded areas like markets and popular tourist sites. Florence's city center is generally safe, but pickpocketing can occur in tourist-heavy spots. A bag with zippers or locks is recommended for peace of mind. If you're planning to capture the beauty of Florence, a camera is an essential item to bring. With its picturesque streets, stunning architecture, and art-filled galleries, you'll want to document every moment. A compact digital camera or even your smartphone with a good camera will be sufficient for most visitors. However, if photography is a passion, don't forget to pack extra memory cards, batteries, and a portable charger to ensure you never miss a photo opportunity. Sunglasses and sunscreen are other essentials to include in your packing, especially if you are visiting during the warmer months. The Florentine sun can be intense, and wearing sunglasses will help protect your eyes from glare while providing comfort throughout the day. Additionally, sunscreen with a high SPF will help protect your skin from the sun's rays while you enjoy the outdoors.

Technology and Essentials for Connectivity: Florence is well-connected, and having the right technology will help enhance your travel experience. If you're traveling internationally, an adapter for European plugs is essential. Italy uses the standard European plug with two round prongs, so bringing an adapter for your electronics is necessary to keep your devices charged. It's also a good idea to bring a portable charger, as you'll likely be using your phone for navigation, restaurant reservations, or language translation apps throughout the day. A SIM card or portable Wi-Fi device is another smart choice for staying connected. You can either buy a local SIM card once you arrive or arrange for an international data plan through your mobile provider. Wi-Fi is widely available in cafes, restaurants, and many public spaces, but having mobile data will allow you to navigate the city and stay connected wherever you are.

Health and Safety Items: When traveling to Florence, it's important to pack items that will ensure your health and safety during your stay. A basic first-aid kit with essentials such as band-aids, antiseptic cream, pain relievers, and any prescription medications you take regularly is a good place to start. If you wear glasses or contacts, be sure to pack spares or an extra set, as it can be difficult to find specific prescriptions while traveling. If you plan on visiting Florence during the peak tourist seasons, or if you have any specific health concerns, packing a refillable water bottle is a great way to stay hydrated while being environmentally conscious. Florence has many public drinking fountains offering fresh, potable water, which is easily accessible around the city. For those concerned about safety, it's advisable to carry a photocopy or digital copy of important documents like your passport, travel insurance details, and emergency contacts. While Florence is generally safe for tourists, it's always good to be prepared in case of an emergency.

Special Items for Food and Wine Lovers: Florence is a paradise for foodies, and if you're passionate about Italian cuisine, there are a few items you might want to pack to make your experience even more enjoyable. If you have a specific diet or food allergies, consider bringing snacks or items that cater to your needs. For example, packing gluten-free snacks or a reusable shopping bag can be helpful if you're planning to shop for local produce in one of Florence's food markets. Wine lovers should also consider bringing a small insulated wine tote if you plan to buy a bottle or two of Florence's renowned Chianti wine to take home. The Italian wine culture is an integral part of Florence, and many visitors enjoy bringing back a bottle of local wine as a souvenir.

9.4 Visa Requirements and Entry Procedures

Those planning a trip to this captivating city, it is essential to understand the visa requirements and entry procedures, which can vary depending on your country of origin. Florence, as a part of Italy, adheres to the rules set by both the European Union (EU) and Schengen Area, so it is important for international travelers to be aware of the specific guidelines they need to follow to ensure a smooth and hassle-free arrival.

Visa Requirements for Florence: For travelers wishing to visit Florence from outside the European Union (EU) or Schengen Area, the first step is to determine whether a visa is required. Citizens of the EU, European Economic Area (EEA) countries, and Switzerland do not need a visa to enter Italy, including Florence, for stays of up to 90 days within a 180-day period. For travelers from other regions, whether or not a visa is needed depends on the country of origin. Citizens of many countries, such as the United States, Canada, Australia, Japan, and several others, can enter Italy for short stays of up to 90 days for tourism, business, or family visits without the need for a visa. This is possible under the Schengen Visa Waiver program, which allows visa-free travel across the entire Schengen Area, of which Italy is a part. For visitors who do require a visa, the process involves applying for a Schengen Visa, which permits travel across all Schengen Area countries for short stays. The visa application process includes submitting required documents such as a valid passport, proof of accommodation in Florence, travel insurance, proof of sufficient financial means, and a return flight ticket. It is highly recommended that travelers apply for their visa well in advance of their trip to ensure enough processing time, which can take several weeks depending on the applicant's country of residence.

Entry by Air: Florence is easily accessible by air through its primary airport, Florence Airport (Aeroporto di Firenze), also known as Amerigo Vespucci Airport. This international airport is located just a few kilometers from the city center, making it one of the most convenient airports for travelers heading to Florence. It handles both international and domestic flights, with a variety of airlines offering services from major cities around the world. When arriving at Florence Airport, travelers will pass through passport control and customs. For those from the Schengen Area or other visa-exempt countries, the process is usually quick and straightforward. However, those arriving from countries that require a visa will need to present their visa documentation along with their passport. It is important to ensure that your passport is valid for at least three months beyond your planned departure from the Schengen Area, as this is a standard requirement for entry. While the airport itself is relatively small, it offers modern facilities and efficient services, making the arrival process relatively hassle-free. After passing through customs, visitors can access a range of transport options to the city center, including taxis, shuttle buses, and car rental services. Florence's historical center is only a short 20-minute drive from the airport, allowing visitors to quickly begin their exploration of the city.

Entry by Train: Florence is well-connected to the rest of Europe by a robust and efficient rail network. The city's main train station, Santa Maria Novella (SMN), serves as the central hub for both domestic and international trains, making it a popular entry point for visitors traveling by rail. For travelers coming from other European cities, such as Rome, Milan, or even Paris, taking a train to Florence is an excellent option that offers both comfort and scenic views of the Tuscan countryside. Trains traveling to Florence from other countries, such as France or Switzerland, are often high-speed trains that provide a smooth and fast ride into the city. Upon arriving at the Santa Maria Novella station, international travelers will need to present their passport and any necessary visa documents at customs control, especially if arriving from non-Schengen countries. As the train station is located just a short distance from the city center, it offers easy access to Florence's key attractions, hotels, and public transportation systems. For those traveling within the Schengen Area, the entry process is typically more straightforward, with little to no checks once passengers disembark from the train. However, for travelers arriving from outside the Schengen Zone, border control may be required upon arrival, depending on the regulations in place at the time of travel. It is important to ensure that all documents, including any necessary visa papers, are readily available to avoid delays.

Entry by Road: For those looking to travel to Florence by car, the city is accessible via an extensive network of highways that connect it to other parts of Italy and Europe. Italy's well-maintained highway system, including the A1 Autostrada, provides easy access to Florence from major cities like Rome, Milan, and Bologna. The city is also reachable from neighboring countries like France and Switzerland, making it a popular destination for road travelers. When arriving by car, there are a few important considerations to keep in mind. Florence's city center is part of a limited traffic zone (ZTL), a restricted area that is closed off to non-residents in order to reduce traffic congestion and preserve the city's historic charm. Visitors should be aware that driving in the ZTL without proper authorization can result in hefty fines. To avoid this, it is advisable to park at one of the city's designated parking areas outside the ZTL and use public transportation or walk into the historical center. For international drivers, it is essential to have a valid driver's license, and in some cases, an International Driving Permit (IDP) may be required, particularly for those from countries outside the European Union. It is always wise to check the latest driving regulations and road signs before embarking on a journey by car.

General Travel Tips and Considerations: Regardless of your mode of travel, it is crucial to have the necessary documents in order before arriving in Florence. This includes a valid passport, any required visas, travel insurance, and proof of accommodation. It is also advisable to keep a copy of all important documents, as well as emergency contact information, in case of any unexpected situations. Florence is a welcoming city that attracts visitors from around the world, and while the entry process is generally straightforward, it is always helpful to plan ahead and be prepared. By understanding the visa requirements and entry procedures for Florence, travelers can ensure that their arrival in this enchanting city will be seamless, allowing them to begin their journey through Tuscany's treasures without delay. Whether arriving by air, train, or road, the experience of stepping into Florence will be one that is unforgettable and full of anticipation.

9.5 Safety Tips and Emergency Contacts

Florence is generally a safe city, especially in the tourist areas, but being informed about safety measures and knowing what to do in case of an emergency is essential. This guide provides key safety tips and emergency contact information that will help you navigate your visit with confidence.

General Safety Considerations for Visitors: Florence is a pedestrian-friendly city with a lot of foot traffic, especially in its historic center. This means visitors should always be vigilant while walking through busy areas, such as the Piazza del Duomo, the Ponte Vecchio, and the Piazza della Signoria, where crowds can become dense. Pickpocketing is a concern, particularly in tourist-heavy spots, so it is advisable to keep your belongings close and secure. Consider using a money belt or keeping wallets and phones in front pockets, as these areas are less vulnerable to theft. If you use a backpack, always keep it in front of you or wear it across your chest when in crowded areas. When exploring Florence's narrower streets or quieter corners, be mindful of your surroundings. Although the city is generally safe at night, as a visitor, it's always prudent to avoid walking alone in poorly lit or isolated areas after dark. Stick to well-populated streets, and always ensure that your accommodation is in a safe part of the city. Florence has a reputation for being relatively safe compared to larger Italian cities like Rome or Milan. Violent crime is rare, but petty crimes, such as pickpocketing and scams, can still occur. Always stay cautious when approached by strangers who seem overly eager to engage with you, especially around tourist landmarks. Common scams in Florence may involve people offering free items or distracting you while an accomplice steals from your bag.

Staying Safe in Transportation and On the Roads: Florence is well-served by public transportation, including buses and trams, making it easy for visitors to explore the city and beyond. However, when using public transit, always be cautious of your belongings. On crowded buses, hold onto your bags and avoid placing valuables in outer pockets or backpacks. If you're renting a bike or scooter to get around, remember that traffic can be hectic, and cyclists need to be aware of both vehicles and pedestrians. Always wear a helmet and follow local traffic rules to avoid accidents. Florence's compact city center is best explored on foot, but if you're planning to rent a car, be aware of the restricted traffic zones (ZTL) within the city. These areas are meant to limit car access to reduce congestion and pollution, and driving into these zones without the proper authorization can lead to hefty fines. If you must drive, make sure to familiarize yourself with the city's traffic laws and parking regulations.

Dealing with Medical Emergencies: While Florence is a relatively safe city, medical emergencies can still happen, and it's important to be prepared. In the event of an accident or sudden illness, Italy's healthcare system is of high quality, and the city has several hospitals and medical centers where you can receive care. The emergency services in Florence are well-equipped to handle a variety of medical situations, and most healthcare professionals are fluent in English, particularly in tourist-heavy areas. If you need medical attention, the first step is to call emergency services. The national emergency number in Italy is 112, which can be dialed for any medical, fire, or police emergency. It is always a good idea to have the address of your accommodation or location on hand, as well as any relevant health information such as allergies or medical conditions. For non-life-threatening medical issues, visitors can head to one of the local pharmacies. Pharmacies in Florence are generally well-stocked with over-the-counter medications, and pharmacists can provide advice for common ailments such as colds, headaches, or digestive issues. Many pharmacies also offer basic first-aid supplies in case you need something simple, like band-aids or antiseptic.

Emergency Services: If you find yourself in a situation where you need immediate assistance, you can contact the emergency services by dialing 112, which connects you to paramedics, police, or fire services. In addition to 112, Italy also has other dedicated emergency numbers. For medical emergencies, you can dial 118, and for police assistance, dial 113. If you lose your passport or wallet, it's crucial to report the loss to the local police. You can do so by visiting the nearest police station, where an officer will take your report and provide a police report, which is essential for canceling credit cards and applying for a replacement passport. The police station closest to the historic center is the Commissariato di Polizia, located on Via Fiume. In case of lost or stolen items, Florence has a lost-and-found service operated by the local police. If you lose something while at a museum, gallery, or public transit, check with the respective location's lost-and-found department. Florence's main train station, Santa Maria Novella, also has a lost-and-found office for any items lost on trains or in the station.

Keeping Emergency Contact Information Handy: Before traveling, it's always a good idea to write down or store emergency contact numbers in a secure place. This includes your home country's embassy or consulate, the local police, and medical services. Most hotels and accommodations in Florence also provide emergency contact information at the front desk, and the staff can assist you with any urgent situations. Having access to your travel insurance information is also crucial, as it can help you handle emergencies more efficiently. Whether you're dealing with a medical issue or lost luggage, your travel insurance can cover many unexpected situations, allowing you to focus on resolving the matter rather than worrying about the costs involved.

9.6 Currency Exchange and Banking Services

When planning a trip to Florence, one of the first practical matters that visitors need to address is currency and banking. Florence, being part of Italy, uses the Euro (€) as its official currency, and understanding the ways to manage money while traveling will enhance your experience in this beautiful city. Whether you're looking to withdraw cash, exchange currency, or use a credit card, there are several banking options available to make these transactions easy and convenient. From local banks to exchange bureaus, Florence is well-equipped to handle the financial needs of international visitors, and this guide will provide all the essential details you need to know about currency, banking, and other money matters during your visit.

Currency in Florence: As the official currency of Italy, the Euro is widely accepted across Florence. Currency exchange rates fluctuate, so it's essential to stay informed about the current rates to ensure you're getting a fair deal. Most international visitors exchange currency at local exchange offices, banks, or ATMs, all of which are readily available around the city. It's also possible to pay with a credit or debit card in most places, including restaurants, shops, and even small cafes, though it's always a good idea to carry some cash for smaller transactions or when visiting places that don't accept cards. While Florence is a modern city, it's important to note that some smaller vendors, particularly in more traditional or remote areas, may prefer cash payments. It's a good practice to always carry a bit of Euro cash with you, especially when shopping in markets or exploring less touristy parts of town. Additionally, always check with your bank before traveling to ensure your credit cards or debit cards will work seamlessly in Italy, as some American cards, for example, might require prior notification to avoid any issues.

ATMs in Florence: ATMs (known locally as "bancomat") are widespread throughout Florence, and they are a convenient way to withdraw cash directly in Euros. These machines are typically found in main tourist areas, near popular attractions, and close to major streets such as Via de' Tornabuoni and Piazza della Repubblica. ATMs are available 24/7, making them ideal for visitors needing access to cash outside of regular business hours. While using an ATM in Florence is generally straightforward, travelers should be mindful of their bank's fees for international withdrawals. Many banks charge foreign transaction fees, and these charges can add up over time, so it's a good idea to inquire about fees before your trip. Additionally, check the exchange rate your bank uses for international withdrawals to ensure it's competitive. Be cautious when withdrawing large amounts of money, as some ATMs have withdrawal limits, and it's also wise to avoid withdrawing from machines located in remote or poorly lit areas for security reasons.

Banks in Florence: For those who prefer handling their finances directly with a bank, Florence boasts several reputable institutions, each offering specialized services for visitors.

UniCredit, located on Via degli Alfani, a central street just a short walk from the Accademia Gallery. UniCredit provides various services such as currency exchange, traveler's checks, and the ability to open short-term accounts for visitors who may need banking services during their stay. They also offer multilingual staff to assist English-speaking customers, making it easier for non-Italian speakers to complete banking transactions.

Intesa Sanpaolo, located near Piazza della Repubblica. This prominent bank offers comprehensive banking services, including currency exchange, wire transfers, and ATMs, making it an ideal place for international visitors to access their funds. Intesa Sanpaolo is known for its customer service and ability to assist travelers with various financial needs, from foreign exchange to more complex banking services.

Banco di Toscana, which operates in the heart of Florence, also offers specialized services for travelers. Located near Piazza del Duomo, this bank provides foreign exchange services with competitive rates and is known for its efficiency and customer-friendly service. Banco di Toscana has a history of serving both locals and visitors, making it a trusted financial institution for those staying in Florence.

Banca Nazionale del Lavoro is another bank with a long history in Italy, offering various banking services to tourists. Located on Via de' Cerretani, close to Santa Maria Novella train station, BNL provides foreign exchange services and financial advice for travelers. Known for its reliability, this bank is a convenient option for visitors who may need assistance with banking while navigating Florence.

Cassa di Risparmio di Firenze, located on Piazza della Signoria, is a local bank that offers tourists not only foreign currency exchange but also additional services like international money transfers and assistance with payment services. Cassa di Risparmio has been a staple in Florence for centuries and offers services tailored to both Italian residents and international guests.

Currency Exchange and Bureaux de Change: If you prefer to exchange currency rather than withdraw cash from an ATM, Florence has a number of reputable currency exchange offices, known locally as "bureaux de change." These exchange centers are scattered throughout the city, especially near popular tourist destinations like the Ponte Vecchio, Piazza del Duomo, and Via del Corso.

Cambio Valori, located on Via della Condotta, offers competitive rates for currency exchange, and it's well-regarded by tourists for its transparency and fair pricing.

Firenze Cambio, situated near Piazza della Repubblica. Known for its efficient service, Firenze Cambio provides currency exchange for most major currencies at competitive rates. It's particularly convenient for tourists who need to exchange cash in a hurry, as it's centrally located and offers a quick turnaround time.

Stazione Santa Maria Novella, the station also features a currency exchange office that operates throughout the day. While airport exchange bureaus can often offer less favorable rates, the one at the train station provides a reliable and convenient option for travelers arriving by rail. It's important to note that while exchange rates at bureaux de change can vary, many of these locations do not charge commission fees, offering a better deal than many hotel exchange services or ATMs. However, visitors should still check the rates to ensure they are getting a fair deal, as some bureaus may offer slightly different rates based on demand or the amount being exchanged.

Managing Money While Exploring Florence: When navigating Florence, it's important to plan your spending in advance. Florence's public transportation system is efficient, with buses and trams that accept contactless payment methods like credit cards, though most tourists prefer to travel on foot to fully experience the city's beauty. Many shops and restaurants in Florence accept credit and debit cards, and ATMs are readily available. However, as mentioned, smaller shops, markets, and vendors may only accept cash, so it's wise to keep a mix of cash and cards with you at all times. Florence is also home to a thriving souvenir market, and while many shops will gladly accept cards, small-scale vendors in markets such as San Lorenzo may prefer cash. When it comes to tipping, it's customary to round up the bill in cafes and restaurants, with a 5-10% tip considered generous.

9.7 Language, Communication and Useful Phrases

Understanding the nuances of its language and communication can significantly enhance your experience. From navigating its winding streets to ordering food in a trattoria, being prepared with some knowledge of Italian and common phrases can transform your trip into a deeply rewarding adventure.

The Language of Florence: The official language spoken in Florence is Italian, which is deeply intertwined with the city's identity and history. As the birthplace of the Renaissance, Florence holds a special place in the evolution of the Italian language itself. It was here that Dante Alighieri, Petrarch, and Boccaccio wrote their masterpieces in a vernacular that later became the foundation of modern Italian. The locals, or Florentines, often speak with a distinct Tuscan accent, which is considered the "purest" form of Italian due to its historical and linguistic roots. Although many Florentines, especially those working in tourism and hospitality, have a good grasp of English, learning a few Italian phrases can go a long way in fostering connections and showing respect for the local culture. Italians appreciate the effort visitors make to speak their language, no matter how basic it may be. This small gesture can open doors to more authentic interactions and often results in a warmer reception from locals.

Communication in a Tourist-Friendly City: Florence is accustomed to welcoming visitors from all over the world, and English is widely spoken in major tourist areas, museums, hotels, and restaurants. In many places, especially those catering to international travelers, menus, signs, and information are often available in English. However, stepping beyond the tourist hotspots into local neighborhoods or less frequented establishments may require some basic Italian.

For those who do not speak Italian, communicating with locals can still be a seamless experience. Most Italians are patient and willing to assist, often using gestures, smiles, and even drawing diagrams if necessary. Florence is a city where body language and expressions play a significant role in communication, so don't hesitate to rely on these universal tools when words fail.

Useful Phrases for Visitors to Florence: Learning a few Italian phrases can enhance your ability to navigate Florence and interact with its people. Whether you're asking for directions, ordering a cappuccino, or expressing gratitude, these phrases are invaluable tools for a traveler. Simple greetings like "Buongiorno" (Good morning) or "Buonasera" (Good evening) help establish a polite tone, while "Grazie" (Thank you) and "Prego" (You're welcome) are essential for everyday exchanges. When asking for directions, phrases such as "Dove si trova…?" (Where is…?) or "Come posso arrivare a…?" (How can I get to…?) will be useful. For dining, knowing how to say "Vorrei…" (I would like…) or "Il conto, per favore" (The check, please) can make the process of ordering food or settling your bill smoother. In the bustling markets, engaging with vendors becomes more enjoyable when you know how to say "Quanto costa?" (How much does it cost?) or "Posso vedere…?" (Can I see…?). Even simple expressions like "Scusi" (Excuse me) or "Mi dispiace" (I'm sorry) can help you navigate crowded streets or interactions with grace.

Cultural Sensitivities in Communication: Florentines are known for their warmth and passion, but understanding cultural sensitivities can make your interactions more meaningful. Respect for traditions and politeness are highly valued, and addressing someone with "Signore" (Sir) or "Signora" (Madam) is considered courteous. When speaking Italian, try to use formal language, especially when addressing older individuals or those in professional roles. It's important to remember that Italians often prefer face-to-face communication and take pride in their conversational skills. Engaging in small talk about the weather, food, or Florence's history can leave a positive impression. However, avoid discussing sensitive topics such as politics or religion unless you are familiar with the person and the context.

Technology and Language Assistance: For visitors who may struggle with the language, technology provides a convenient solution. Translation apps like Google Translate can help bridge the gap, offering instant translations for both text and speech. Many apps also allow users to download Italian language packs for offline use, ensuring that you're equipped to communicate even without internet access. Additionally, several digital phrasebooks and language-learning apps are available to help you familiarize yourself with Italian before and during your trip. These resources can be especially helpful for practicing pronunciation and building confidence in using the language.

Embracing the Language of Florence: Ultimately, language is more than just a tool for communication; it's a way to immerse yourself in Florence's vibrant culture and history. By making an effort to learn and use Italian phrases, you'll find yourself connecting more deeply with the city and its people. Whether you're engaging in casual conversations with locals, haggling for souvenirs, or simply exchanging pleasantries, the effort you put into embracing the language will be met with appreciation and goodwill.

9.8 Shopping and Souvenirs

Florence is also a treasure trove of shopping opportunities. From elegant boutique stores to quaint antique shops, the city offers an enchanting mix of modern sophistication and timeless charm. For visitors seeking unique souvenirs or indulgent shopping experiences, Florence provides an abundance of options scattered throughout its picturesque streets and vibrant districts. With this guide, you'll discover remarkable shopping destinations in Florence, each offering distinct goods and unforgettable experiences.

LuisaViaRoma: LuisaViaRoma, an iconic boutique store located on Via Roma near Piazza della Repubblica, is a must-visit for those in search of high-end fashion and accessories. Renowned for its curated selection of designer brands such as Gucci, Prada, and Balenciaga, LuisaViaRoma caters to fashion enthusiasts who appreciate both luxury and innovation. Visitors can browse through the store's collection of clothing, handbags, footwear, and jewelry, each piece reflecting contemporary trends and meticulous craftsmanship. Prices at LuisaViaRoma are reflective of its luxury status, with items ranging from €200 for accessories to over €3,000 for designer apparel. The store opens its doors daily from 10:00 AM to 7:30 PM, offering ample time to explore its opulent displays. Conveniently located in the heart of Florence, it is easily accessible by foot from most central hotels or by using public transportation to Piazza della Repubblica.

Antica Fonderia del Bronzetto: For a more traditional shopping experience, Antica Fonderia del Bronzetto on Via Romana is a delightful stop. Specializing in antique bronze items, this shop boasts a collection of exquisite home decor pieces, sculptures, and artisanal lamps that embody Florence's rich artistic heritage. Each item is handcrafted, making it a unique souvenir for anyone captivated by history and craftsmanship. Prices at Antica Fonderia del Bronzetto vary based on the complexity and size of the pieces, with smaller items like candleholders starting at €50 and larger sculptures reaching several hundred euros. The shop is open Monday through Saturday, from 9:30 AM to 6:30 PM. Located near the Boboli Gardens, the store is accessible by a short walk from the city center or via local bus routes that stop nearby.

Mercato Centrale: For a lively and colorful shopping experience, Mercato Centrale is an unmissable destination. Located on Piazza del Mercato Centrale in the San Lorenzo district, this bustling market is a haven for food lovers and souvenir seekers alike. The ground floor is filled with stalls selling fresh produce, cheeses, meats, and spices, while the upper floor hosts a variety of artisanal food vendors and specialty shops. Visitors can purchase locally made olive oils, wines, and handmade pasta—perfect gifts to bring the flavors of Florence back home. Prices at Mercato Centrale are generally affordable, with small food items like jars of truffle sauce or packets of dried pasta starting at €5, while bottles of premium Tuscan wine can range from €15 to €50. The market operates daily from 8:00 AM to midnight, making it a convenient stop for both early risers and night owls. Located just a short walk from Santa Maria Novella train station, it is easy to reach on foot or by public transportation.

Scuola del Cuoio: Scuola del Cuoio offers a unique shopping experience dedicated to Florence's renowned leather craftsmanship. This historic workshop and store produce an array of handmade leather goods, including bags, wallets, belts, and jackets. Visitors can witness artisans at work, making each item a testament to Florence's centuries-old leatherworking tradition. Prices at Scuola del Cuoio reflect the quality of the craftsmanship, with smaller items like wallets starting at €50 and larger items such as leather jackets reaching €500 or more. The store is open Monday to Saturday from 10:00 AM to 6:00 PM. Located near the Arno River, it is a 15-minute walk from the city center or easily accessible by bus routes that stop near Piazza Santa Croce.

Il Papiro: For those who appreciate the beauty of handcrafted paper goods, Il Papiro on Via del Parione is a delightful boutique. Specializing in Florentine stationery, the shop offers journals, notebooks, decorative paper, and writing accessories, all created using traditional methods of marbleized paper making. Each item is a blend of functionality and artistry, making it a thoughtful gift or keepsake. Prices at Il Papiro are accessible, with small items like bookmarks and postcards available for under €10, while larger items like journals and writing sets range from €20 to €50. The store is open daily from 10:00 AM to 7:00 PM. Located near Piazza Santa Trinita, it is within walking distance of major attractions and is easily reached via public transportation.

9.9 Health and Wellness Centers

Florence also offers an array of health and wellness centers that provide visitors with a chance to unwind, rejuvenate, and focus on their well-being. From luxurious spas to holistic wellness centers, Florence's diverse options allow visitors to enhance their physical and mental health while enjoying the beauty and tranquility that the city has to offer. Whether you're seeking a luxurious spa treatment, a wellness retreat, or an innovative fitness center, Florence's health and wellness offerings cater to every need.

Spa and Wellness at the Four Seasons Hotel Florence: The Four Seasons Hotel Florence, known for its unparalleled luxury, houses one of the city's finest wellness centers. Located in a magnificent Renaissance palace surrounded by beautiful gardens, this exclusive spa offers a serene and elegant environment for visitors seeking relaxation and rejuvenation. The spa at the Four Seasons provides a comprehensive range of treatments, including traditional massages, aromatherapy, facials, and signature treatments that use locally sourced ingredients such as olive oil and wine, both renowned for their health benefits. In addition to the standard spa services, the Four Seasons also offers fitness facilities, a heated indoor pool, and yoga classes. Whether you're looking for a quick refresh after a day of sightseeing or a full-day spa experience, this wellness center provides the perfect escape from the bustling city. The hotel's tranquil garden setting adds an extra layer of relaxation, making it a peaceful retreat in the heart of Florence.

FloWellness: For those interested in a more holistic approach to health and wellness, FloWellness is an excellent option. Located in the heart of Florence, this wellness center specializes in both physical and mental well-being through a combination of therapies designed to treat the body, mind, and spirit. FloWellness offers a variety of services, including yoga classes, pilates, mindfulness meditation sessions, and reiki healing. The center also provides personalized nutrition advice and detox programs to support your body's natural healing processes. Guests can indulge in deep tissue massages, reflexology, and other treatments designed to relieve stress and tension. FloWellness is an ideal spot for visitors who want to focus on a balanced, healthy lifestyle during their time in Florence. The center's peaceful and nurturing environment encourages a sense of tranquility, making it a perfect place for those looking to reconnect with their inner selves while exploring the cultural riches of Florence.

The Spa at Villa Cora: The Spa at Villa Cora, nestled in a historic 19th-century villa on the hills overlooking Florence, offers a luxurious and refined wellness experience. This spa combines old-world elegance with modern wellness techniques, making it a top destination for visitors seeking relaxation and beauty treatments. The spa features a range of treatments, from revitalizing body wraps and massages to facials designed to nourish and rejuvenate the skin. Guests can enjoy the wellness area, which includes a Turkish bath, a sauna, and a large outdoor swimming pool with a stunning view of the city. What makes this spa particularly unique is its location: surrounded by lush greenery and offering an idyllic, peaceful atmosphere, the spa provides an escape from the city's hustle and bustle while being just a short distance from Florence's historic center. Whether you're in need of a pampering facial, an indulgent massage, or simply a place to relax in luxurious surroundings, Villa Cora's spa promises to meet your every need.

Asmana Wellness World: Asmana Wellness World, located just outside of Florence, offers an expansive and immersive wellness experience that's unlike any other in the city. This wellness center is a haven for those looking to combine relaxation with a unique sense of adventure. Asmana is one of Italy's largest wellness centers, featuring a vast range of saunas, thermal baths, and relaxation areas spread across more than 10,000 square meters. The center boasts a variety of themed saunas, including Finnish, Roman, and Himalayan salt saunas, each providing a different therapeutic experience. In addition to the saunas, guests can enjoy outdoor thermal pools, whirlpools, and quiet relaxation zones with panoramic views of the Tuscan countryside. Asmana also offers a variety of massages and beauty treatments, ensuring a complete wellness experience. The center's extensive facilities make it an excellent destination for visitors who are looking for a day of indulgence and relaxation. It's a place where you can completely unwind, recharge, and enjoy the benefits of thermal waters in a serene and tranquil setting.

Centro Benessere Il Girasole: Centro Benessere Il Girasole is a holistic wellness center located in the heart of Florence that emphasizes the healing power of nature. This wellness center offers an extensive range of services focused on natural health treatments, including massage therapy, beauty treatments, acupuncture, and energy healing. One of the standout features of Il Girasole is its dedication to creating personalized wellness plans for each visitor, taking into account their unique health concerns and personal goals. The center is known for its commitment to sustainable and eco-friendly practices, using organic and locally sourced products in its treatments. Centro Benessere Il Girasole also offers various wellness workshops and classes, including mindfulness, meditation, and natural beauty routines, aimed at helping visitors lead healthier lives both during their trip and beyond. For those looking to explore alternative forms of healing, this wellness center is a must-visit, offering a peaceful and calming space for rejuvenation.

9.10 Useful Websites, Mobile Apps and Online Resources

These tools provide everything from detailed maps and public transport information to insider tips on dining, sightseeing, and hidden gems. Whether you're planning your itinerary, looking for real-time information, or simply navigating the city, these digital resources will be your trusted companion.

The Florence Tourist Information Website: The official Florence tourist information website is one of the most important resources a visitor can have at their disposal. This website offers a wealth of information about the city, including detailed descriptions of major attractions, museums, galleries, and historical sites. Whether you're looking to book tickets to the Uffizi Gallery, find out about the best walking tours, or learn about local events happening during your stay, this website has it all. It also provides practical travel information, such as public transport timetables, visitor guidelines, and helpful tips on local customs, allowing you to plan your trip more efficiently. In addition to the wealth of practical information, the site offers interactive maps and event listings, making it easy to access the latest cultural happenings around Florence. This website is essential for any traveler looking to understand the layout of the city and the must-see experiences while also discovering less-visited spots that might otherwise be overlooked.

The Florence Pass App: For those keen on seeing as much as possible during their time in Florence, the Florence Pass app is an essential tool to have. This app simplifies the process of exploring the city's iconic attractions, offering a one-stop solution for ticket booking, museum reservations, and audio-guided tours. It allows visitors to purchase tickets for top attractions like the Uffizi Gallery, the Florence Cathedral, and the Accademia Gallery directly from their smartphones, skipping the long queues. Additionally, the app offers real-time updates on the availability of tickets, special exhibits, and opening hours, helping travelers make the most out of their time. It also includes maps of the city, highlighting key points of interest and providing route suggestions, ensuring that you never miss out on the must-see spots. The Florence Pass app is especially helpful for those who wish to prioritize their time and avoid the hassle of waiting in line, offering a convenient and streamlined experience for tourists.

Google Maps: Google Maps remains one of the most versatile and widely used mobile apps for visitors navigating Florence. Whether you're walking, using public transportation, or even driving, Google Maps offers detailed, real-time directions to help you get from one place to another. With the app's ability to pinpoint specific destinations, provide walking routes, and offer suggestions for nearby restaurants or shops, it becomes an invaluable tool for daily exploration. Google Maps also includes street view images, so visitors can preview iconic sights like the Ponte Vecchio or the Florence Cathedral before visiting them in person. Beyond basic navigation, Google Maps also provides helpful reviews and ratings of restaurants, bars, and shops, allowing you to make informed decisions while in the city. Additionally, the app is constantly updated with the latest traffic information, public transit schedules, and any road closures or changes, ensuring you can always find the quickest and most efficient routes during your stay in Florence.

Tripadvisor: When it comes to discovering local dining gems, hidden attractions, and authentic experiences in Florence, Tripadvisor is one of the most reliable mobile apps available. Known for its vast user-generated reviews, Tripadvisor allows travelers to gain insights into the best places to eat, stay, and visit, based on feedback from real visitors. The app features detailed descriptions, photos, and reviews for everything from Michelin-starred restaurants to casual trattorias serving delicious Tuscan cuisine. In addition to dining recommendations, Tripadvisor covers local attractions, excursions, and even guided tours, offering ratings and advice from past visitors. The app also includes practical features such as the ability to book tours, make restaurant reservations, and create personalized itineraries, all from within the app. Whether you're looking for a traditional Florence dining experience or seeking something off the beaten path, Tripadvisor offers honest reviews and up-to-date suggestions to enhance your visit.

Rome2Rio: For visitors planning to explore Florence and its surrounding regions, the Rome2Rio app is a fantastic resource. Rome2Rio is a travel planning tool that provides real-time information on how to get from one location to another, whether it's within Florence or to nearby cities like Pisa, Siena, or Rome. The app covers a variety of transportation methods, including trains, buses, taxis, and even flights, making it easy to plan day trips or multi-destination journeys. Rome2Rio gives you options for routes, travel times, and estimated costs, helping you choose the most convenient and cost-effective way to move around. This app is particularly useful for visitors who want to explore the Tuscan countryside, visit vineyards, or explore other towns in the region. It ensures that visitors are well-informed about their travel options, helping them navigate the complex Italian transport system with ease.

9.11 Internet Access and Connectivity

Florence draws millions of tourists each year. For many travelers, staying connected while navigating the city's maze-like streets or booking tickets for museums and tours is essential. Fortunately, Florence offers a variety of internet access and connectivity options that cater to the diverse needs of international visitors. From public Wi-Fi hotspots to mobile data services, there are plenty of ways for travelers to stay online while enjoying all that this enchanting city has to offer. Understanding the different options available will ensure that your stay in Florence is both enjoyable and digitally connected.

Public Wi-Fi Hotspots Across Florence: Florence, like many major tourist cities, has made efforts to enhance public internet access through a network of Wi-Fi hotspots. These hotspots are scattered throughout the city, especially in key tourist areas, making it convenient for visitors to stay connected while exploring the city's iconic landmarks. The Comune di Firenze (City of Florence) has set up several public Wi-Fi points in high-traffic areas such as Piazza del Duomo, Piazza della Signoria, and Piazza Santa Croce, ensuring that visitors can easily access the internet while resting or waiting at these famous spots. These public networks are ideal for travelers who need to check maps, browse for restaurant reviews, or get directions while on the go. The Wi-Fi networks in these areas typically require users to sign up with their email or register through a simple online form. The connection is free, though some hotspots may have limitations on session times or the bandwidth speed. Visitors will find that these hotspots are usually sufficient for light browsing, checking emails, or using social media. However, for more data-intensive tasks, such as streaming videos or large downloads, a more robust option like mobile data may be preferable.

Overall, Florence's public Wi-Fi hotspots are an excellent option for staying connected while enjoying the city's rich cultural offerings.

Hotel and Accommodation Wi-Fi: For travelers who prefer a more reliable and uninterrupted internet experience, most hotels, hostels, and other accommodations in Florence offer complimentary or paid Wi-Fi. Hotels range from luxurious five-star properties to budget-friendly guesthouses, and most provide internet access in their rooms and public spaces, such as the lobby or business center. While high-end hotels often offer premium internet services with faster speeds and greater bandwidth, more budget-conscious accommodations may provide basic Wi-Fi that is suitable for casual browsing and social media updates. Before booking a place to stay, it's a good idea to verify the Wi-Fi availability and service quality. Many hotels in Florence advertise free Wi-Fi, but it's essential to check for any restrictions on usage, such as limits on the number of devices that can connect at once or slow speeds in certain areas of the hotel. If staying at an Airbnb or other rental property, the host will typically provide information about the Wi-Fi, but it's wise to confirm the service quality beforehand. For visitors who require a stable internet connection for work or long video calls, upgrading to a business hotel or considering coworking spaces with high-speed internet access may be more suitable.

SIM Cards and Mobile Data Plans: For those who need continuous internet access throughout their trip, purchasing a local SIM card or a mobile data plan is a highly recommended option. Italy has several mobile network providers that offer affordable and flexible data plans for tourists. Major carriers such as TIM, Vodafone, WindTre, and 3 Italia operate in Florence and offer various prepaid SIM cards designed for short-term visitors. These cards can be purchased at any mobile phone shop or at designated kiosks at Firenze Santa Maria Novella train station and the Florence Airport. Once a SIM card is purchased, travelers can activate it and start using mobile data for internet access immediately. Depending on the plan, SIM cards typically come with a specific amount of data, and prices can vary based on the amount of data included and the validity period. Prepaid plans usually offer competitive prices, with options ranging from daily, weekly, or monthly packages. These plans allow for unlimited browsing, social media use, and navigation, making them a convenient option for travelers who need access while moving around the city. Moreover, having a local SIM card ensures that visitors have internet access even in areas outside the city center, where public Wi-Fi might not be available.

Coworking Spaces with High-Speed Internet: Florence is home to several coworking spaces that cater to both digital nomads and visitors who need a more professional and reliable internet connection. These spaces offer high-speed internet, comfortable workstations, and a collaborative atmosphere, making them ideal for anyone looking to work remotely or simply stay connected for extended periods. Popular coworking spots like Regus Florence, The Florence Hub, and Firenze Coworking provide day passes or flexible membership options for visitors who need temporary access to an office environment. These coworking spaces not only offer fast and secure internet but also provide additional services such as printing, meeting rooms, and networking opportunities with other professionals. The spaces are designed to be comfortable and conducive to productivity, making them perfect for travelers who need to catch up on work while in Florence. For those on a short-term visit, using a coworking space can be an excellent solution for maintaining consistent internet access, especially if your accommodation does not provide sufficient Wi-Fi for work-related tasks. Additionally, many coworking spaces in Florence are located near popular tourist areas, so they are easy to reach when you need a break from sightseeing and need to focus on work or personal projects.

Internet Cafes and Public Access Computers: Though less common in many modern cities, **internet cafes** are still available in Florence, providing an option for travelers who may not have a personal device or SIM card with mobile data. These cafes are equipped with public access computers that offer internet services for a small fee. Visitors can use these cafes to check emails, browse the web, or book travel tickets. While internet cafes are not as widely used today due to the prevalence of mobile data and Wi-Fi availability, they can still be found in areas frequented by tourists, such as near Piazza della Repubblica or Piazza del Duomo. Most internet cafes offer an hourly or per-minute rate for computer usage, and the charges are typically affordable. Some cafes also provide printing services, which can be helpful for travelers who need to print out boarding passes, tickets, or travel itineraries. Additionally, internet cafes may offer a place to relax and enjoy a coffee while staying connected to the world online. While they may not be as convenient as using your own mobile data or hotel Wi-Fi, internet cafes offer an alternative solution for staying connected when traveling in Florence.

9.12 Visitor Centers and Tourist Assistance

Florence has a range of well-established visitor centers and specialized tourist assistance services designed to ensure a smooth and enriching experience for every traveler. These services cater to the diverse needs of visitors, whether they are looking for maps, booking tours, or simply seeking local recommendations. Understanding the various options for visitor support will help enhance your visit and ensure that you don't miss any of Florence's treasures.

The Florence Tourist Information Center (IAT): One of the most prominent and centrally located tourist information centers in Florence is the Florence Tourist Information Center (IAT). Located in the heart of the city, just steps away from the iconic Piazza del Duomo, this center serves as the first point of contact for many visitors. Situated at Piazza San Lorenzo, 6, the center offers a comprehensive range of services designed to assist tourists in making the most of their time in Florence. Upon entering, you'll find a team of multilingual staff ready to provide guidance on everything from the best sightseeing spots to information on local public transportation. The Florence Tourist Information Center specializes in offering city maps, brochures, and detailed guides to popular attractions such as the Uffizi Gallery, the Florence Cathedral, and the Ponte Vecchio. They also provide information on special events, exhibitions, and festivals happening around the city. For those seeking to book guided tours, the IAT center offers reservations for both group and private tours, including tours of museums and walking tours of historical sites. Moreover, the center has an assortment of guided tours available in multiple languages, ensuring that visitors from around the world can easily explore Florence. The center also offers tips on navigating the city efficiently, recommending the best routes to take, and even providing advice on lesser-known attractions that are not often featured in typical travel itineraries.

Florence Airport Tourist Assistance: For travelers arriving in Florence by air, the Florence Airport Tourist Assistance service is a valuable resource. Located directly at the Aeroporto di Firenze Peretola, this center is situated in the main terminal, making it easily accessible as soon as you land. The airport assistance service is equipped to offer tourists detailed information on transportation options from the airport to the city center, which is located about 4 kilometers away. Whether you prefer to take a taxi, shuttle bus, or rent a car, the staff at the tourist assistance desk can guide you through the most convenient and cost-effective options. In addition to transport guidance, the airport center provides a variety of essential services for visitors. These include brochures about the city's key attractions, helpful information on local cultural events, and assistance in booking tickets for museums and galleries. The Florence Airport Tourist Assistance desk also provides maps of the city, offering useful tips on how to get around Florence, especially for first-time visitors who may find the maze-like streets challenging to navigate. Multilingual staff are available to assist travelers, making it easy for non-Italian speakers to access relevant information and services.

The Florence Visitor Center at Santa Maria Novella Station: Another vital resource for travelers is the Florence Visitor Center, located inside the Santa Maria Novella Railway Station. Situated at Piazza della Stazione, 1, this visitor center is strategically placed for those arriving by train, which is one of the most popular modes of transportation in Italy. Florence's train station is a major hub, and the visitor center inside is a convenient stop for anyone arriving in the city by rail. The Santa Maria Novella Visitor Center provides tourists with a wealth of useful services, including information about public transportation, suggestions for day trips from Florence, and tips on nearby attractions that are often overlooked by tourists. Visitors can also purchase tickets for various museums and attractions directly at the center, bypassing long lines at the entrances. Additionally, the center offers personalized advice and helps visitors tailor their itineraries based on their interests. Whether you're looking for a guided tour of the historic city center or recommendations for local restaurants, the knowledgeable staff at the Santa Maria Novella Visitor Center are happy to assist.

Tuscany Tourist Information Center: For those looking to explore Florence in the context of the larger region of Tuscany, the Tuscany Tourist Information Center is an excellent option. Located at Via Cavour, 61, just a short walk from the Florence Cathedral, this center offers in-depth advice and services for visitors interested in exploring more than just the city itself. Tuscany, renowned for its stunning landscapes, vineyards, and charming medieval towns, is a treasure trove of experiences, and the Tuscany Tourist Information Center specializes in providing guidance for these excursions. This center is ideal for travelers looking to organize day trips to places like Pisa, Siena, or the Chianti wine region. The staff at the Tuscany Tourist Information Center can assist in booking tours, arranging transportation, and providing itineraries for those wanting to explore beyond Florence. They also offer maps and pamphlets on regional attractions, from art galleries to hidden countryside gems, making it the perfect place to plan a broader Tuscan adventure. In addition to its tourism services, the center frequently hosts workshops and cultural events that allow visitors to immerse themselves further in Tuscan culture.

Palazzo Vecchio Tourist Assistance: For those interested in diving deeper into Florence's rich artistic and cultural history, the Palazzo Vecchio Tourist Assistance desk is an excellent resource. Situated in the heart of Florence, within the Palazzo Vecchio, this visitor assistance service is located at Piazza della Signoria, 1. Palazzo Vecchio, a stunning medieval town hall, is one of Florence's most iconic landmarks, and the visitor center here provides information on this historic building as well as the city's broader cultural offerings. The staff at the Palazzo Vecchio Tourist Assistance desk are knowledgeable about Florence's history, and they offer valuable insights into the museum's exhibitions and the history of the building itself. Visitors can access information about ticket prices, tour options, and opening hours for Palazzo Vecchio and other nearby attractions like the Uffizi Gallery and the Pitti Palace. Additionally, the center assists in organizing private tours and provides suggestions for visitors who are looking for exclusive experiences, such as private viewings of galleries or behind-the-scenes tours of historical sites.

Tourist Assistance: In addition to the visitor centers scattered throughout the city, Florence offers various specialized services designed to improve the overall experience of travelers. These services include mobile apps for navigating the city, audio guides for exploring major attractions, and personalized concierge services for visitors looking for a more tailored experience. Florence's tourist assistance network also includes walking tours, bike rentals, and even services for travelers with special needs. Whether you're a first-time visitor or a seasoned traveler, the wealth of information and assistance available ensures that navigating Florence's charming streets and discovering its treasures is an experience to remember.

CHAPTER 10
EVENTS AND FESTIVALS

10.1 Overview of Florence's Events and Festivals

Florence is not only a hub for art and history but also an exciting destination for the fashion-forward. The Pitti Uomo Fashion Week, held every year in June, stands as a beacon of innovation and style. This prestigious event, one of the most prominent in Italy, draws designers, buyers, and fashion enthusiasts from across the globe to witness the cutting-edge collections of menswear. The event takes place at the stunning Fortezza da Basso, a historic fortress in the heart of Florence, which is transformed into a bustling center of creativity. The Pitti Uomo is not just a fashion showcase but also a celebration of Florentine craftsmanship, with its array of side events that highlight the city's long-standing tradition of tailoring, leatherwork, and luxury accessories. For fashion lovers, it's a chance to experience the convergence of global style and timeless Florentine elegance. Getting to the event is quite convenient, as Fortezza da Basso is located near the Santa Maria Novella train station, making it accessible to travelers arriving by rail. Entry to the fashion shows typically requires an invitation, but the surrounding events, such as exhibitions and pop-up shops, can be enjoyed by the general public, often with free entry. However, for those wishing to access the exclusive runway shows, tickets may be available upon request or through invitation only. If you're fortunate enough to secure a spot, you'll be in for a truly immersive experience in the world of fashion.

Festa della Rificolona: Florence takes on a magical atmosphere every September 7th during the Festa della Rificolona, a centuries-old festival that brings the streets alive with colorful lanterns, music, and festivities. This event, rooted in the Renaissance era, celebrates the Virgin Mary's birth and is one of the city's most cherished traditions. The festival's highlight is a grand procession that takes place in the evening, where children and adults alike carry beautiful, hand-crafted paper lanterns, known as "rificolone," through the narrow streets of Florence. The procession makes its way toward Piazza Santissima Annunziata, where the culmination of the celebration includes music, street performances, and the lighting of fireworks that paint the night sky. For visitors, the festival offers a delightful glimpse into the local culture and community spirit. The rificolone are often handmade by local artisans, making them not only colorful but also an excellent souvenir. Visitors can join in the fun by purchasing their own lanterns, often found at street vendors around the city center. The event is free to attend, and you'll find the streets of Florence filled with excitement, joy, and a sense of camaraderie. If you happen to be in Florence during early September, don't miss out on this enchanting festival, which immerses you in the heart of Florentine tradition.

Scoppio del Carro (Explosion of the Cart): One of the most exhilarating and dramatic events in Florence is the Scoppio del Carro, which takes place every Easter Sunday. This ancient tradition, dating back to the 15th century, involves the spectacular explosion of a cart filled with fireworks. The event is meant to ensure a good harvest for the year and is believed to bring prosperity and good fortune. The cart, or "carro," is drawn by a team of oxen from Porta al Prato to the Piazza del Duomo, where a ceremonial ignition takes place during the high Mass at the Cathedral of Santa Maria del Fiore. As the cart explodes in a brilliant display of fireworks, the entire city holds its breath, waiting for the fuse to ignite, symbolizing the safety and prosperity of the coming year. Visitors flock to Florence in April to witness this awe-inspiring spectacle. The event is open to the public and free of charge, though arriving early is advisable to secure a good vantage point. The Scoppio del Carro is an experience that transcends time, blending centuries of Florentine history and tradition with the excitement of modern-day celebrations. It's an unmissable occasion for those who are lucky enough to be in Florence during Easter.

Maggio Musicale Fiorentino: For music lovers, the Maggio Musicale Fiorentino is a must-see event. Held annually from April to May, this world-renowned music festival features a dazzling lineup of operatic performances, orchestral concerts, and chamber music. The festival takes place at the stunning Teatro del Maggio Musicale Fiorentino and other venues throughout the city, offering a rich program that attracts the world's leading composers, conductors, and musicians. The festival's performances are often accompanied by the Florence Opera, and some of the best-known opera singers grace the stage, making it a true celebration of classical music. The Maggio Musicale Fiorentino is more than just a series of concerts; it's an opportunity to immerse yourself in Florence's deep connection to the arts. The performances are typically held in the evenings, and tickets can be purchased online or at the venue. While some concerts may be on the expensive side, there are often discounted tickets or special packages for students or young people. For those seeking a cultural experience rich in musical heritage, the Maggio Musicale Fiorentino is an unforgettable way to explore the city's artistic soul.

Florence's Feast of San Giovanni: Florence's Feast of San Giovanni, held on June 24th, is a lively celebration dedicated to the city's patron saint, St. John the Baptist. This grand event combines religion, history, and entertainment in a way that only Florence can. The day begins with a solemn religious procession, where the city's most important churches participate, and the streets are lined with spectators eager to catch a glimpse of the participants. As the day progresses, the celebrations take a more festive turn with the traditional calcio storico – a historic football match that dates back to the 16th century. This intense game, which combines soccer, rugby, and wrestling, is played in the Piazza Santa Croce and is a thrilling spectacle for spectators. The day culminates with a magnificent fireworks display along the Arno River, lighting up the sky in a riot of colors and offering a perfect end to the day's festivities. Visitors to Florence on June 24th can join in the celebrations by attending the religious processions or catching the fireworks along the riverbank, both free of charge. For those seeking a more immersive experience, watching the calcio storico live is an unforgettable way to witness the passion and history of Florence firsthand. The Feast of San Giovanni is a day to celebrate Florence's rich history and culture, and it's an event that will leave you with lasting memories of this beautiful city.

10.2 Must-Attend Events

The Maggio Musicale Fiorentino is one of Florence's most anticipated cultural events, encapsulating the city's passion for music and opera. Held every year from late April to early May, this festival is a dream for anyone with an appreciation for world-class performances. Imagine yourself stepping into the grand Teatro del Maggio Musicale Fiorentino, where the sounds of an orchestra fill the air and voices of operatic divas soar to the heavens. The festival, which spans several weeks, features a captivating blend of operas, symphonic concerts, and ballet performances, often bringing together renowned artists from around the world. Attending the Maggio Musicale Fiorentino is an unforgettable experience, but getting there is fairly straightforward. The Teatro del Maggio Musicale Fiorentino is located near the Cascine Park, easily accessible by tram or bus from the city center. For visitors arriving by car, there is parking available around the venue, though public transport is highly recommended for convenience. Depending on the specific performance, ticket prices can vary, but expect to pay between €20 and €150 for most events, with discounts available for students and senior citizens. Be sure to check the festival's official website for the full schedule and to book tickets in advance, as some shows tend to sell out quickly. Whether you're an opera aficionado or simply someone who appreciates spectacular performances, the Maggio Musicale Fiorentino will make you fall even deeper in love with Florence's cultural allure.

Pitti Immagine Uomo: Florence's rich history is mirrored in its prominence in the world of fashion, and Pitti Immagine Uomo is the ultimate celebration of men's style. Held biannually in June and January, this prestigious event draws the most influential designers, buyers, and media from around the globe to the Fortezza da Basso. The event is a hub of cutting-edge fashion, with some of the best Italian and international designers presenting their latest collections. However, Pitti Immagine Uomo is more than just a fashion show—it is an immersive experience. Visitors can wander through the exhibition halls, where top brands display their innovative creations and artisans show off their bespoke craftsmanship. If you're passionate about the world of fashion, you'll find yourself captivated by the sheer creativity that defines this event. To get to Pitti Immagine Uomo, the Fortezza da Basso is located just a short walk from Florence's main train station, Santa Maria Novella, making it easily accessible for both locals and tourists. Entry to the event is typically restricted to industry professionals, but for those with an invitation or accreditation, attending offers unparalleled access to the world of high fashion. However, the city also offers a vibrant street style scene during the event, where even those without official tickets can see the fashion-forward crowd strut around the city. While the event itself doesn't have a set entry fee, private showings and exclusive parties may require special invitations or a fee for admission. If you're in Florence during one of these iconic fashion weeks, experiencing Pitti Immagine Uomo will leave you breathless with its dazzling array of style.

The Florence Film Festival: Cinema lovers flock to Florence each year for the Florence Film Festival, an event that celebrates both the art of film and the beauty of the city itself. Typically held in March, this festival showcases a curated selection of independent films from both Italian and international filmmakers. With a focus on innovation and artistic vision, the Florence Film Festival gives filmmakers an opportunity to present their work to an enthusiastic and diverse audience. In addition to the films, the festival often hosts workshops, panel discussions, and Q&A sessions with directors, actors, and other industry professionals. For film buffs, this is a golden opportunity to immerse yourself in the world of cinema and witness new talent pushing the boundaries of storytelling. The festival's main venue is usually the Cinema Odeon, a historic theater that exudes old-world charm. Situated in the heart of Florence, this venue is easily accessible by foot or public transport. The atmosphere inside the cinema is intimate, allowing you to experience films in a way that few other venues can offer. Ticket prices for the Florence Film Festival vary depending on the screening, but most films are priced between €8 and €12, with discounts for students and seniors. The festival's website provides detailed information on the schedule and ticket availability, so visitors can plan their visit accordingly. Whether you're an aspiring filmmaker or simply someone who loves watching stories come to life on the big screen, the Florence Film Festival promises to be a remarkable journey into the world of cinema.

Festa della Rificolona: The Festa della Rificolona, held every year on September 7th, is one of Florence's most beloved traditions, bringing together locals and visitors in a lively celebration of history, culture, and light. Originating in the Middle Ages, this festival marks the eve of the Nativity of the Virgin Mary, and it is most famous for its colorful procession of lanterns. Children, families, and even adults walk through the streets of Florence, carrying hand-made lanterns crafted from paper and glass, creating a spectacular display of lights that illuminates the city. The atmosphere is joyful and festive, with music, food, and traditional games adding to the excitement. The best way to experience the Festa della Rificolona is by joining the procession, which typically begins in the late afternoon and continues well into the evening. The main route winds through the historic center, passing by some of Florence's most iconic landmarks, including the Duomo and Piazza della Signoria. Entry to the event is free, making it a great option for those on a budget. However, if you're looking for a special experience, you can book a table at one of the many local trattorias or restaurants along the route, where you can enjoy a traditional Florentine meal while watching the festivities unfold. The event is a true feast for the senses, and the sight of the city's streets bathed in the glow of hundreds of lanterns will remain etched in your memory long after you leave.

Scoppio del Carro: Held every year on Easter Sunday, the Scoppio del Carro (Explosion of the Cart) is one of the most unique and exhilarating events in Florence. This centuries-old tradition takes place in Piazza del Duomo and is a stunning spectacle that combines history, religion, and fireworks in a way that is unlike any other. The event begins with the procession of a massive cart, which is pulled through the streets by a team of oxen and loaded with fireworks. The cart is brought to the cathedral, where the mayor of Florence uses a special dove-shaped rocket to ignite the cart's fireworks. What follows is an impressive display of fireworks that lights up the sky, symbolizing good luck and prosperity for the city. The Scoppio del Carro has its roots in medieval times, and its connection to Florence's rich history is part of what makes it so captivating. The best vantage points to watch the event are along the perimeter of Piazza del Duomo, though the crowds can be quite large. The event is free to attend, though be prepared for busy streets as locals and tourists alike flock to the square. For those who wish to enjoy the spectacle in comfort, there are also private viewing opportunities available at nearby restaurants and hotels, but these often require advance reservations. Whether you're a fan of fireworks or simply curious about local traditions, the Scoppio del Carro will leave you awestruck by its dramatic display of color and fire.

10.3 Hidden Gems of Events and Festivals
The Scoppio del Carro, or the Explosion of the Cart, is one of Florence's most unique and visually spectacular events, held annually on Easter Sunday, typically in early April. This historic celebration has roots in medieval traditions and is a thrilling way to experience the city's vibrant culture. The spectacle is centered around a massive cart, the "Carro," which is filled with fireworks and drawn through the city by a team of oxen. The cart is then ignited in front of the

Cathedral of Santa Maria del Fiore (Florence's Duomo), with the hope that the ignition will signal a good harvest for the year. Visitors are treated to an explosion of colors and sounds, as the fireworks burst into the sky, filling the air with excitement and a sense of ancient ritual. To attend, simply arrive in Piazza del Duomo early in the morning, as the event takes place right outside the cathedral. While the event itself is free, it is advisable to arrive early to secure a good viewing spot, as this event attracts both locals and tourists. Florence's streets become particularly crowded on Easter, so be prepared for large crowds and limited transportation options. If you're planning to stay in the area, consider booking accommodations early as this is a popular event. The spectacle offers a chance to witness Florence's deep-rooted traditions, with a palpable energy that makes it an unforgettable experience.

Florence Tango Festival: The Florence Tango Festival, held each June, is a magical gathering for dance enthusiasts from all corners of the globe. This festival celebrates the Argentine tango in all its passionate glory, transforming Florence into a vibrant dance hub. With world-class tango dancers and musicians performing in iconic locations such as Piazza della Signoria and the Palazzo Vecchio, this event is a true feast for the senses. The festival's workshops, where both beginners and seasoned dancers can improve their skills, are equally popular. Whether you're a tango aficionado or simply someone who enjoys watching graceful performances, the Florence Tango Festival offers something special for everyone. Getting to the event is relatively simple—most of the festival's activities are centered around the city's main piazzas and historic venues, all within walking distance of each other. The festival offers free access to many of its open-air performances, but you may need to buy tickets for certain workshops or more exclusive tango events. These tickets can usually be purchased online in advance or at the festival's designated ticket offices. Florence's warm June evenings create the perfect atmosphere for dancing under the stars, with the city's architectural beauty providing a stunning backdrop to the sultry steps of the tango.

Festa della Rificolona: One of the lesser-known but equally enchanting festivals in Florence is the Festa della Rificolona, celebrated every year on September 7th. This event is a celebration of the Virgin Mary's Nativity, and it's marked by a procession of children carrying colorful paper lanterns, known as "rificolone." The streets of Florence are illuminated with hundreds of these homemade lanterns, creating a magical atmosphere as the children march through the historic city center. The procession ends in the Piazza del Duomo, where the lanterns are gathered and a lively festival atmosphere ensues, complete with traditional music, food stalls, and local vendors. This festival is an excellent opportunity to experience Florence like a local. While the event itself is free, it's customary to purchase a rificolona lantern from one of the stands lining the streets, helping to support this centuries-old tradition. Visitors can enjoy the festivities by following the procession through the heart of Florence, enjoying the warm September evenings and the charming medieval streets. Getting to the event is easy, as it takes place in the historical center of the city, close to major landmarks like the Duomo and the Palazzo Vecchio. For those looking for a more immersive experience, you may want to try making your own lantern at one of the local workshops, a unique way to engage with the culture of Florence.

Calcio Storico: The Calcio Storico, or Historic Football, is a fierce and ancient game that is still played in Florence today, with its roots tracing back to the 16th century. Held annually in June, this event takes place in the Piazza Santa Croce, where teams representing the four historical districts of Florence—Santa Croce, San Giovanni, Santa Maria Novella, and Santo Spirito—compete in this brutal, no-holds-barred version of soccer. The game is a mix of soccer, rugby, and wrestling, with little regard for the usual rules of sportsmanship, making it a thrilling event to witness. If you're lucky enough to be in Florence during the Calcio Storico, you'll find the entire city buzzing with excitement. The final match, which takes place on June 24th, marks the feast day of Saint John the Baptist, the patron saint of Florence. The streets surrounding the Piazza Santa Croce are filled with spectators, while the match itself takes place inside a makeshift arena. While the event is free to attend, getting a good seat requires patience, as the piazza fills up quickly. Be sure to arrive early to grab a spot. If you're interested in the historical significance of the event, guided tours of the district offer additional insight into this centuries-old tradition.

Festa di San Giovanni: Festa di San Giovanni, held on June 24th, is the ultimate celebration of Florence's patron saint, Saint John the Baptist. This festival is marked by a spectacular fireworks display that lights up the Arno River and the Florentine skyline, as well as a historical football match known as Calcio Storico. While the fireworks show is the highlight of the evening, the day is filled with various cultural events, including parades, concerts, and religious ceremonies. The festival's grand finale is the iconic fireworks display, set off from the banks of the Arno River, offering a breathtaking view of the city's bridges, buildings, and the Duomo, all illuminated against the night sky. The event takes place in the heart of Florence, and like most Florentine festivals, it is accessible to everyone. The fireworks are visible from various points along the riverbanks, but the best views can be had from Piazzale Michelangelo, a hilltop spot that overlooks the city. While the fireworks are free to watch, attending the full festivities, including the Calcio Storico match, may require purchasing tickets. Be prepared for crowds, as this event is immensely popular among both locals and tourists. It's advisable to plan your visit to Florence well in advance, especially if you want to be part of the action and avoid the large crowds that gather around the main event locations.

10.4 Cultural Events and Exhibitions
Each of these cultural events and exhibitions adds a unique layer to the experience of visiting Florence. Whether you're a fashion aficionado, an art lover, a music enthusiast, or someone who seeks to immerse themselves in the traditions of the city, these events provide the perfect opportunity to witness the vibrancy and cultural richness of Florence in every season. Each event is a reflection of the city's deep respect for its past while embracing the ever-evolving world of contemporary creativity. They offer visitors a chance to engage with Florence in a way that is both intimate and expansive, promising unforgettable memories and experiences.

Firenze4Ever: Held every January, Firenze4Ever is one of the most anticipated cultural events in Florence, offering a unique intersection of fashion, art, and digital culture. This exclusive event is organized by the renowned fashion retailer LuisaViaRoma and takes place at their flagship store in the heart of Florence. The event brings together leading global influencers, designers, and artists for a celebration of luxury fashion intertwined with artistic performances and installations. Throughout the event, attendees are treated to immersive exhibitions that feature collaborations between top fashion brands and contemporary artists, creating a visual feast that ignites the imagination. The setting of Firenze4Ever is nothing short of magical. As the store becomes a hub for cutting-edge fashion and avant-garde exhibitions, the city's architectural beauty provides an unforgettable backdrop. Walking through the event feels like stepping into an art gallery, where every corner reveals a new fashion creation, often paired with interactive displays that allow guests to engage with the pieces. The event is by invitation only, so while access to the exhibition itself may be exclusive, the experience is invaluable for those lucky enough to attend.

To make the most of this occasion, visitors are encouraged to plan their stay in advance and explore not only the event but also the surrounding historical sites. With no direct entry fee for the exhibitions, the cost usually comes with participation in the fashion shows and related exclusive events.

Florence Biennale: Every two years, Florence becomes a beacon for contemporary art enthusiasts as the Florence Biennale transforms the city into a vibrant celebration of modern creativity. Held in the fall, typically in October, this prestigious event showcases the works of international artists in various mediums, including painting, sculpture, photography, and digital art. The Biennale provides a platform for both emerging and established artists to present their works to a global audience. The exhibitions are held at the Fortezza da Basso, a historic site that perfectly complements the contemporary art on display, creating a fascinating juxtaposition between Florence's storied past and the cutting-edge present. The Florence Biennale is an immersive experience that invites visitors to explore the works of artists from around the world while also taking in the cultural richness of the city. With galleries spread across multiple exhibition halls, the event fosters a dynamic atmosphere, where creativity and innovation are on full display. For those interested in participating, there are usually entry fees that allow access to the exhibitions and related events, such as artist talks and panel discussions. The event attracts a diverse crowd, from seasoned art collectors to curious tourists seeking to engage with contemporary art in one of the most artistically rich cities in the world. Visitors can also explore the surrounding streets of Florence, where the city's heritage meets the future of global art. The event serves as a reminder that Florence is not only the cradle of Renaissance art but also a thriving hub for modern and contemporary artistic expression.

Festa della Rificolona: Every September 7th, Florence comes alive with the Festa della Rificolona, a unique cultural celebration that blends tradition, light, and local pride. This festival, deeply rooted in the history of Florence, marks the eve of the Nativity of the Virgin Mary. The streets of Florence are illuminated with colorful paper lanterns, crafted by local artisans, creating a stunning visual spectacle that draws both locals and tourists into its embrace. The Rificolona festival has been celebrated since the 12th century, and over the centuries, it has evolved into a joyous and lively event that encompasses parades, folk music, and traditional dances. As the evening falls, the streets are filled with people carrying their handmade lanterns, often in the form of animals or symbolic shapes. The sound of folk music fills the air, and children play traditional games, making the festival an unforgettable experience for families. The atmosphere is electric with excitement, as locals and visitors alike participate in the procession, winding through the historic city center towards the Piazza del Duomo, where the festival culminates in a beautiful display of lights. Entry to the event is free, but the experience is priceless. Visitors can also indulge in local delicacies sold at street food stalls, adding a flavorful dimension to the visual and cultural feast. The Rificolona is a testament to Florence's ability to celebrate its ancient traditions while making them accessible and enjoyable for everyone.

Opera di Firenze: The Opera di Firenze, Florence's premier opera house, hosts an impressive array of cultural events throughout the year, offering a sophisticated experience for those passionate about music, theater, and the performing arts. The venue, located near the Cascine Park, hosts performances ranging from classic operas and ballets to modern musical theater and symphonic concerts. The opera season typically runs from October through May, with a calendar packed with performances that attract world-renowned artists and conductors. For opera lovers, attending a performance at the Opera di Firenze is a must. The building itself is a modern architectural marvel that provides excellent acoustics, enhancing the experience of live performances. Whether you are enjoying a grand opera or an intimate ballet, the ambiance of the venue transports visitors into a world of classical music and timeless performances. Tickets for performances vary in price depending on the production, but for many, the opportunity to witness the finest operatic talent in one of Europe's most culturally rich cities is worth every penny. Additionally, the opera house offers educational programs and masterclasses, allowing aspiring artists to immerse themselves in the world of professional performing arts. It is an essential stop for anyone seeking to experience the cultural heartbeat of Florence in its most refined form.

Maggio Musicale Fiorentino: Every spring, Florence hosts the Maggio Musicale Fiorentino, one of Italy's most prestigious music festivals, drawing thousands of visitors to the city. Held in May, this month-long event celebrates the city's rich musical heritage and contemporary performances. The festival is known for its world-class opera productions, orchestral concerts, and ballet performances, featuring renowned international artists and conductors. The Maggio Musicale Fiorentino is a testament to Florence's long-standing commitment to the arts, providing a platform for both classical music and contemporary works. The festival's performances take place at various venues across the city, with the main stage being the Opera di Firenze. Each year, the festival's program is a carefully curated selection of operatic masterpieces, symphonic concerts, and innovative productions. Visitors to Florence during the Maggio Musicale Fiorentino can expect a cultural experience like no other, where music fills the air and the city itself seems to come alive with the rhythm of the performances. While the festival features performances of international acclaim, it also provides opportunities for local artists to showcase their talents. Entry fees vary depending on the production, but the opportunity to experience world-class music in such an iconic city makes this festival a highlight for any visitor. The Maggio Musicale Fiorentino offers a deep dive into Florence's musical soul, providing an unforgettable cultural experience that will resonate long after the final notes fade.

10.5 Music and Dance Events
The Florence Dance and Music Festival is one of the most anticipated events in the city, offering a mesmerizing blend of performances that capture the rich cultural heritage of Italy. Held each year in June, this vibrant festival transforms the city into an open-air theater, with performances taking place in some of Florence's most iconic outdoor spaces. The Boboli Gardens, with its timeless beauty and lush landscapes, is often chosen as the setting for many performances, giving the festival an enchanting atmosphere. Visitors are invited to experience an unforgettable combination of classical and contemporary music, ballet, and theatrical performances, which make the Florence Dance and Music Festival a must-see event for art lovers. The festival is not just about the performances themselves but also about the immersive experience of being part of the city's cultural fabric. Whether you're watching a ballet dancer gracefully move under the stars or listening to an orchestra playing Mozart's finest pieces, the whole event captures the essence of Florence's artistic spirit. Entry fees vary depending on the performance and location, with tickets generally ranging from €20 to €50, making it accessible to a wide range of visitors. To attend, it's best to arrive early to secure the best spots, especially if you plan to attend a performance in the Boboli Gardens, which can fill up quickly due to the breathtaking views. For those new to Florence, public transport offers easy access to many of the festival's venues, with the Santa Maria Novella train station being a central point for getting around the city.

Maggio Musicale Fiorentino: Held annually in May, the Maggio Musicale Fiorentino is Florence's premier classical music festival. For over eight decades, this prestigious festival has attracted top-tier orchestras, soloists, and conductors from around the world, and it continues to be a major highlight in the city's cultural calendar. The festival, which typically spans the entire month of May, celebrates the very best in opera, orchestral music, and chamber performances. It is held at the grand Teatro del Maggio Musicale, which has been a cultural hub for Florence since 1930. The festival is an unmissable experience for music lovers, with opera lovers in particular being drawn to the opera performances staged at the theater, many of which are directed by world-renowned conductors and feature stunning vocal performances. The event also includes symphonic concerts, recitals, and chamber music sessions, allowing for an all-encompassing musical experience. It is not only about the performances but also about the atmosphere that Florence's theaters create, where the city's historical and artistic significance converges with contemporary performances. Tickets for the Maggio Musicale Fiorentino vary, ranging from €30 to €150 for premium seating, and tickets can be purchased through the official festival website. For those arriving by public transport, the Teatro del Maggio Musicale is easily accessible from various parts of the city via bus and tram services, with the nearest stop being "Stazione Leopolda," located just a short walk from the venue.

Firenze Jazz Festival: For lovers of jazz music, the Firenze Jazz Festival, held every July, is an exceptional event that brings together some of the finest jazz musicians from around the world. The festival is a celebration of improvisation and creativity, capturing the spirit of jazz in one of the most captivating cities in the world. The performances take place across various venues in Florence, including intimate clubs, grand theaters, and open-air locations, making the festival an inclusive event for all jazz enthusiasts. The highlight of the Firenze Jazz Festival is undoubtedly the performances by internationally acclaimed jazz musicians, who perform alongside emerging talents in unique collaborations. The city itself becomes the backdrop for a vibrant exchange of musical styles, blending traditional jazz with modern interpretations. Entry fees for the festival vary depending on the performance, with many of the smaller venue performances priced around €20, while larger concerts in places like the Teatro Verdi may cost upwards of €40 to €60. Visitors can easily reach these venues by public transportation, with the Santa Maria Novella station being a central hub for accessing the festival's locations. The charming streets of Florence also come alive during the festival, with jazz musicians often performing in cafes and on street corners, giving the city an even more magical feel.

Florence Folk Festival: The Florence Folk Festival, typically held in late summer, is an explosion of music and dance that highlights the diverse folk traditions of Italy and the world. Each August, the festival gathers folk musicians, dancers, and performers from various countries, offering a unique opportunity to witness global traditions in one of the most charming cities in Europe. The performances, which take place in public squares, theaters, and outdoor spaces, feature a blend of traditional folk music and contemporary interpretations of cultural heritage, drawing crowds from all over the world. What makes the Florence Folk Festival so special is its interactive nature. Visitors can enjoy performances by folk musicians, and many of the events include opportunities for guests to participate in workshops and learn traditional dances or music. The city's most iconic locations, such as the Piazza della Signoria and the Santa Croce Square, host open-air performances where visitors can join the festivities. Entry fees for the Florence Folk Festival are usually affordable, with many events being free or priced at €10 to €30 for tickets. The festival's central locations are easily accessible by public transport, with buses and trams connecting major squares and venues throughout Florence. Attending the Florence Folk Festival is a celebration of cultural exchange and community, making it a memorable experience for those eager to discover the diversity of world music and dance.

Opera di Firenze Summer Season: During the summer months of June and July, Florence hosts the Opera di Firenze Summer Season, a premier event that brings together the grandest productions of opera and classical music. Held at the stunning Teatro dell'Opera di Firenze, the summer season attracts opera lovers and music enthusiasts from all over the world, offering a chance to experience iconic operatic works in one of the finest opera houses in Italy. The summer season often includes grand productions of famous operas by composers like Verdi, Puccini, and Mozart, staged with elaborate sets, world-class singers, and cutting-edge productions that showcase the theater's rich history and modern capabilities. The Opera di Firenze Summer Season is not just about watching performances; it is about immersing oneself in the grandeur and drama of opera. The performances, held in the Teatro dell'Opera di Firenze, a state-of-the-art venue, provide an unforgettable sensory experience, where the beauty of the music is matched only by the incredible acoustics and stunning architecture of the opera house. The cost of tickets for the Opera di Firenze Summer Season ranges from €25 to €100 depending on the seat and the production. Tickets can be purchased online or at the venue's box office.

CONCLUSION AND RECOMMENDATIONS

As you prepare to leave the heart of Italy, the city that has inspired artists, poets, and dreamers for centuries, Florence will undoubtedly have left an indelible mark on your soul. The narrow, cobbled streets echo with the whispers of the past, from the grandeur of the Duomo to the timeless elegance of Michelangelo's David. Each corner of this Renaissance jewel offers a chance to witness history and art in the making, a city that feels both timeless and utterly alive. Florence is not merely a destination; it's an experience, one that will stay with you long after your journey ends. But as you immerse yourself in Florence's magic, there are a few secrets and insider tips that can enhance your visit, taking it from memorable to extraordinary. These are the subtle, yet powerful, insights that only those who have truly embraced the city can offer. By tapping into these recommendations, you'll not only discover the must-see landmarks but also uncover the hidden gems that make Florence so special.

Secret Gardens and Tranquil Corners: While the city is famous for its iconic squares and museums, Florence is also home to hidden oases of calm. One such place is the Bardini Garden. Just a short walk from the Pitti Palace, this lush garden offers sweeping views over the city and the Arno River—without the usual hustle and bustle. As you wander through the terraced paths, you'll feel as though you've stepped into a different era. The garden's quiet beauty, filled with fragrant roses, ancient olive trees, and sculptures, provides the perfect respite after a busy morning of sightseeing.

The Real Taste of Florence: Florence is a paradise for food lovers, but to truly experience the soul of Tuscan cuisine, you must venture beyond the tourist-centric restaurants around the Duomo. Head to the Oltrarno district, just across the Arno River, where locals dine in unassuming trattorias and family-run eateries. One such spot is Trattoria Sostanza, known for its iconic butter chicken (pollo al burro)—a dish so simple yet rich in flavor that it will forever change the way you think about comfort food. The real magic, though, is in the ambiance: intimate, cozy, and filled with the warm chatter of Florentine families. Don't forget to try lampredotto, a traditional Florentine street food that is an acquired taste but will definitely add a layer of authenticity to your journey.

Explore Florence's Artisan Shops: Florence is a city where craftsmanship and creativity intertwine. As you wander through its winding streets, seek out the artisan workshops where Florentine traditions are kept alive. The Via de'

Tornabuoni is home to some of the world's most luxurious shops, but just a few steps off this grand avenue, you'll find small, family-owned leather shops and goldsmith ateliers. Look for Scuola del Cuoio near Santa Croce, where you can watch artisans crafting leather goods by hand. If you're looking for a unique souvenir, this is where you'll find high-quality leather products that carry the spirit of Florence.

The Best Views of Florence (Without the Crowds): Florence's panoramic views are legendary, and while most tourists flock to Piazzale Michelangelo for a sunset view, there's another spot that will reward those who know where to look. The Rose Garden, Giardino delle Rose, just below Piazzale Michelangelo, offers stunning vistas over Florence, especially during the golden hour. Not only will you enjoy the cityscape, but you'll also be surrounded by vibrant roses in full bloom—an atmosphere that's perfect for a moment of quiet reflection. It's an idyllic spot, often overlooked by tourists, which makes it all the more enchanting.

Timing Your Visit to Florence's Famous Attractions: When it comes to Florence's most popular sites, timing is everything. For the Florence Cathedral, skip the long queues by pre-booking your tickets for early entry. If you're keen on climbing the Dome, plan to go either at sunrise or close to sunset, when the light softens, casting an ethereal glow over the city. Similarly, the Accademia Gallery, home to the magnificent David, is often busiest around midday. Aim for a visit right when it opens, and you'll have the opportunity to admire Michelangelo's masterpiece in peace.

Florence is not just a place to visit—it's a city to fall in love with. Its charm doesn't just lie in its historical landmarks or world-class art; it's in the details—the scent of freshly baked bread wafting through the air, the quiet conversation of artisans at work, the laughter spilling out from trattorias as the evening unfolds. Every corner has a story, and every moment holds the potential for discovery. For those willing to embrace its rhythms, Florence offers not only a window into the past but a lasting imprint on your heart.

Printed in Great Britain
by Amazon